A WAYWARD

SPIRIT

By Peter J. Harris

Part One: The World Beckons ...

Part Two: Peace, Tranquility, Enlightenment

(The extraordinary experiences of a globe-trotting business executive who discovered a spiritual world and changed his life)

(Edited by Peter Marshall)

EDITOR'S FOREWORD

Working on this book has revealed the lifetime experiences of Peter Harris – an 'ordinary bloke' with a hyper-active drive to travel the world and with an extraordinary series of stories to relate. They range from the successes and failure of his business life to his mid-life discovery of a spiritual dimension and belief, and a personal and often critical insight into the workings of 'religion'.

All this comes from a treasure trove, in the form of a 'Pandora's' box file containing pages of hand-written notes. These were composed contemporaneously over the years during his visits to no less than 109 countries. But these pages, hand-written on random letterheads, contain so much more in the way of Peter's innermost thoughts, saved in the box with a traveller's collection of press cuttings, photos and souvenirs.

I began asking myself how could so much happen to one man? I can only say that there is nothing but truth and insight – and humour- in the events he has described.

His stories fall naturally into two sections – but which overlap chronologically. At first he was describing vividly the remarkable events which befell him on his business travels in many parts of the developing world as he sought to promote first the British travel industry and then the educational opportunities to 'learn English in England'. Over these years, in his own words, he was a wayward spirit. But then came the beginnings of his spiritual enlightenment and his involvement with retreats, religions and a search for a deeper meaning to his life. This has now led him into diverting his seemingly limitless energies into charity work in Asia, with more remarkable stories to relate.

Purists may question the mixture of tenses in the course of this book. I have done this (without explanation) to preserve the original narrative of sections which Peter recorded in his hand-written notes.

Read on! All will be revealed ...

Peter Marshall

A WAYWARD SPIRIT

By Peter Harris

"WRITE SMALL BOOKS" – SAID MURTHY

I've always been a somewhat wayward spirit, acted impulsively and been driven to many corners of the world; but then I saw that the riches of spirit had been paramount and I found the desire to pull down the brick walls which surrounded and limited me (and probably most of us). Any failure can become a moment of grace, words that ring true in our lives however many rocks have been thrown across our paths. The trouble is that most of us only appreciate the transformation that's taken place in retrospect.

I spent ten years of my life building up a chain of schools in Australia and New Zealand. Four schools and all was before me, as I had the financial backing of one of the oldest travel and tour operators in New Zealand. I did it all on a shoestring, ploughed in all my available cash and all seemed rosy until the crash of '89 when the travel company was taken over, sold off with all its subsidiaries and I was left owning four schools with money seeping away as though I was a colander. I didn't listen to my own intuition and my inner being and heed the warning that pride goes before a fall.

In 2002, and many adventures later, I was told about a palm reader by a German doctor and was determined to see him on my next visit to India. According to Indian tradition, everybody's palm may be interpreted by a good reader who can tell you about its life and past lives. The palm reader, Murthy, was apparently highly regarded and respected. I found him in Bangalore in a small, whitewashed room with an exposed light bulb dangling in the middle.

I told him my age, 54 years, ten months and 22 days. He then proceeded to tell me about my upbringing and my three children. He said I had experienced a previous life in India as a follower of the Shri Sai Baba (a divine guru with paranormal powers according to his followers). There I had learned ayurvedic medicine and meditation and had voyaged in China as a teacher of martial arts, as well as being in New Zealand and Egypt. I was born in England as a navigator and would travel the world for knowledge and writing. However, I wasn't suited to England, he said; I had powerful hands and I needed to channel that power for writing small books.

Mankind is carried along on a frenetic conveyor belt of hype and illusion, assuming that all can be achieved by the acquisition of material wealth. Now, I cannot and never will submit to such thinking. Peace of mind for many comes through silence, the ability to stop the monkey brain. Give and you shall receive, as the saying goes.

If we were all driven by the same desire to know our inner selves as we are to make money what a wonderful world it would be. Since time began, we have all needed shepherds to lead us; now we have politicians who can't conserve and look after the world's resources, but feel a constant need to plunder them. Why not look for alternative sources of energy? We cannot and should not rape the environment. Man must look into his heart and speak candidly.

I've just finished reading *Tomorrow's God*, by Neale Donald Walsh, which was awe-inspiring and reinforced my view that as humanity we need to find another way. In essence we are all one and most religious groups claim ownership of God rather than accepting that they have their path and that other paths are equally as valid. Religion for many youngsters is boring and uninspiring with no relevance in their eyes. There is a lack of realization that the godhead is within us all; enlightenment to me is each individual finding his or her own spiritual path - we don't need to belong to a fashionable group and be led like sheep. All the answers that we need are within us. Love and joy are paramount. We've all been conditioned by an educational process which to many people seems like an exam conveyor belt. We are not inspiring youngsters to create; we teach, they learn, it is rarely a two way process. All of my kids are far superior to me in the use of the DVD and what you can do with a mobile phone and computer. I'm still in the dark ages and in their eyes have fond memories of quill pens.

Many people worldwide are restless, dissatisfied with their political rules and searching for a more meaningful existence. We are taught to consume, accumulate and not share. The Englishman's home is his castle and beware anyone who crosses the ramparts. Many people within the UK are innately racist, but it's not a subject we talk about now; however, there is a realization that we have a lot to learn from our Indian community about family values. I saw a wonderful film recently, *Wondrous Oblivion*, which was about a West Indian family who moved in next to a Jewish family and the various conflicts and joys they went through before a true understanding emerged.

We are who we are, we must listen to our hearts and be honest within ourselves. Once we've climbed one mountain, we must be prepared for the next.

It is always difficult to know where to start a story of one's life. It is important, I believe, to give up one's dependency and throw away the tentacles of society that envelop and suffocate one's being. Get back to nature, be grounded, enjoy the rhythm of the seasons. Change occurs through awareness, like a sail boat with a full head of wind, moving effortlessly, but sails need tending and boats need steering. Finally, I feel I have slowed down and can taste and smell. I have let all my senses become alive.

So many of us live empty, soulless lives because we crave popularity, appreciation, and praise, and have lost contact with sunsets, good books, good movies, enjoyable work and good company.

I remember sitting at a dinner party with all the props and trappings of business success, thinking that something was terribly lacking in my life and I genuinely could not put my finger on it. Over dinner we talked about a vast range of topics and somebody asked if I had heard of Mother Meera. It transpired that eight out the 12 people there had all been to see her. I was hooked, though I wondered how an Indian guru, based in Germany, who at the time had written one book, *Answers*, could attract to her people from middle class countries?

When I found her, there was silence and power... and what joy! Mother Meera, even to the cynical, had an aura which is palpable and as she enters the room there is electricity. One sits for up to two hours at Darshan meditating, clearing what Sai Baba would call 'the monkey brain'; then one kneels before her and there is a laying-on of hands. The experience each time is very different. Mother Meera obviously brings great joy and substance to many, sends us out into the ever-changing world with a new perspective, having adjusted our balance. May tolerance prevail over ethnocentric views. I feel in a way as though I've come full circle, my batteries are charged, I'm on an even keel and more able to accept what life throws at me, *carpe diem*, enjoy life, do good, be compassionate, these are thoughts that prevail in my subconscious... the search continues along another path, one door closes, another opens and so it is important to pass on before one becomes too cynical, while one can openly embrace change.

But first, let me take you back to some of my character-forming earlier years and experiences...

Travel has and does play an extremely important part in my life and looking back that might seem strange for someone who was brought up in a Dorset village which had one bus into town for market day. The limit of our family holidays was camping in Cornwall at Coverack – like so many people in the '50s and '60s. My sister Jilly always had a yen to leave the hedgerows and thatched cottages of Dorset and in fact she emigrated to New Zealand when she was 18 and I was 14.

I first went abroad on a visit to Austria as a reward for passing the much-maligned 11-plus exam but the roller coaster only began for me at the age of 17 when I volunteered for VSO (Voluntary Service Overseas) and spent a year in Rhodesia at a Catholic, French-speaking mission, 80km into the 'bundu' at Kutama – where its most famous old boy is one Robert Mugabe. It always staggered me that no other African leaders decried his actions in later years.

Life has been a rich voyage ever since – being shot at in San Salvador, held hostage in Khomenei's Teheran and capsized in Cyclone Alison in Australia. Life is a constant learning curve; curiosity drives me and most things can be overcome by humour – which we sometimes sadly lose when we need it most.

It never ceases to amaze me how there are coincidences in life. In 2014 I was asked at the last moment to give a speech at a BAISC (British Association of International Study Centres) annual conference dinner in Birmingham. I had been given little prior warning – in fact I arrived back from Bangkok on the morning of the conference. First, my taxi to the airport in Bangkok was involved in a traffic accident, and being a foreigner I had to pay! (It reminded me of an American in Saudi Arabia whose taxi went through green lights and was hit by another car – he was arrested on the basis that he was an infidel and if he had not been in the country the accident would not have happened). Then my bags were lost by BA and ended up in Africa. I arrived for my speech in time but with no notes, so I scribbled on a serviette the names of a number of countries I had visited when marketing British education internationally over a period of some 30 years and used that for my rambling exposé. It was very well received and this prompted me to put pen to paper. I had previously tried writing about my experiences and also asked various friends to supply me with interesting travel stories; my aim was to compile a book for Danny Fewtrell, a gifted sportsman hit by cancer, but with an indomitable spirit, and who has proved to be one of the major inspirations in my life.

Most of the anecdotes I collected were interesting but my idea did not work out– and so the onus has now fallen on me to continue the task and, as Murthy suggested "to write small books". But I would also like to thank Norman Harris, Trev Williams, Mark Mathews and fellow Turkish Parrots for their contributions to this book; and my editor, Peter Marshall, for pulling together my random jottings into what I hope is a more readable compilation.

10

PART 1 - THE WORLD BECKONS

EARLY TRAVELS AND A CYCLONE AT SEA

As I didn't pass maths or physics at O-level I failed to matriculate for university and spent a year with VSO in Rhodesia. On my arrival at Kutama Mission I was met by the Abbot. They were French-speaking Catholics who spoke little to no English. He gave me a forked stick and a torch because they had a problem with poisonous snakes in the rainy season. I needed to check the pathways at night and my clothes in the morning. It was my first real experience of cultural shock. Within a 20-mile radius of Kutama there were 13 other Missions ranging from the Baptists to the Seventh Day Adventists and I am sure that a lot of young Africans were mobile in their devotion as there was constant competition for converts.

Whilst I was there the Fathers had to sell their mission house in Salisbury (now Harare) because one of the Fathers with a PhD from Oxford was black, thus we were forced to move into a multi-racial area in town. The entrenched attitudes and bigotry gave me very little desire to return to the country or South Africa. Because Ian Smith declared UDI, I left the country early in February 1965.

On arriving home my father asked me if I would like to join my sister Jilly and her husband Dennis on their drive across North Africa and down to Addis Ababa. Dennis had previously cycled to India with a chum in '64, met my sister at the Tokyo Olympics then hitched back from India... quite some trip. They were leaving in March and he would give me the money he was keeping for my twenty-first. I jumped at the chance and spent three happy months driving across North Africa with a man who was to become a major influence in my life. We were turned back in the Sudan because of the fighting twixt the Arabs and Christians. I got a deck passage from Alexandria to Piraeus and they headed for Baghdad. I sold blood and my camera in Athens to garner enough money for the train fare to Vienna. I met a group of GI's on they train and told them my story so they gave me their leftover food and had a whip round to pay the rest of my fare home. Thereafter I trained as a teacher at St Luke's College, Exeter which, in the mid-60's, was changing from men only to mixed and offered a stimulating social and sporting life.

My first teaching position was at Oldfield boys' school in Bath, which was next to the main railway line and the students caught double decker buses to the playing fields which were three miles away. The gym at the school was unsafe and couldn't be used. The Head was a small Welshman and when school assemblies were held in the Hall he couldn't be seen or heard from the constant noise of the railway drowning out his words. On my first day checking the register I was told to f*** off twice by two of the more challenging students. I taught mainly migrant children and one Chinese lad's only English was the menu of his parent's fish and chip shop; another had been used as a dartboard by his father and had lost an eye. It was a blackboard jungle on all fronts and my biggest challenge was maintaining a sense of order and discipline, especially when I took them on visits to museums and art galleries to broaden their cultural experiences as they were apt to run wild.

At the end of my first year's teaching I capsized a sailing boat in a sewage outlet near Lulworth Cove in Dorset and ended up spending six weeks in the Isolation Hospital in Weymouth which certainly brought me closer to my father who visited regularly. On recovery I applied for a teaching job in New Zealand and was accepted as long as I completed a degree whilst teaching. I spent four very happy years there playing rugby, skiing, sailing, socialising and enjoying all the country had to offer. The school was another world. The boys wore boaters, stood when you walked into class… worlds apart from my previous experience.

I was second-in-command of the Naval Cadets and this gave me the opportunity to develop my love of sailing. When I finished my degree I joined a crew delivering a boat from New Zealand to Tasmania, via Sydney and discovered that cabin cruisers don't hold up particularly well in Southerlies blowing through the Fouveaux Straits – especially when one windscreen wiper fails to function and you have to take hand-held bearings of the clumps of rock which suddenly appear out of nowhere. But we arrived, in an exhausted state, delivered the boat – and I then got a job as a concrete labourer on a building site – which was a marked change from teaching at one of the leading schools in New Zealand.

At the first 'smoko' we had to elect a union rep and as I was the only person who could either speak English or say anything without using the 'f' word as the sole adjective I was duly elected and given an office in a Portakabin from which I set about representing my colleagues with a certain vigour and zeal, much to the dismay of management.

I was able to save a tidy sum and took off for Coff's Harbour in New South Wales where I had been asked to skipper a boat to Singapore. When I got there, two couples were on board – an engineer and his wife and a doctor and his girlfriend. Later we were joined by a South African and a Swedish girl. The 64ft ferro-concrete ketch had been built by the doctor and the engineer in their back garden. They had never been out of Sydney Heads Harbour before sailing up to Coff's Harbour - their first step on what was planned to be a round-the-world trip.

We left the harbour in calm conditions and I was bemused by the fact that the two people who had built this ketch were actually planning to sail around the world. They listened to the local pop station for weather forecasts and their navigational knowledge hadn't allowed for the possibility of a 15degree variation in their location in the Tasman Sea. Basically, with this level of seamanship, they should never have been at sea at all; it's a bit like those sailors who leave Auckland in NZ and turn left on the basis that they will hit Australia somewhere.

After two days at sea there were cyclone warnings. Cyclone Tracy had already demolished Darwin and Cyclone Akusa was heading across the Tasman for Fiji! Lo and behold it changed course and headed towards us. I had never been anywhere near a cyclone before. The sea rotates, as does the wind, waves were crashing over the mast 32 feet above the deck and we were lashing ourselves to the mast to give the boat some head; we had no sails up, some engine and a storm jib out. The two retired owners were below with violent sea sickness and I was left to take over with a South African crew member to keep the boat afloat. Our food below deck was swamped and after five days of this I was hallucinating as the sharks, which normally came up for the fish flooded down by the rivers, began to circle ominously. It was like something out of a terrifying novel.

We managed to gradually creep closer to the shore and I could see the flashing lights of Byron Bay. Before collapsing through exhaustion, I told one of the girls on board to steer us in, keeping starboard of the flashing light; she didn't, she went to port and grounded the boat on a surf beach. The owners by this time had come back up on deck, and were attempting to re-float the boat. It was like being in a washing machine. They had taken the channel against my wishes and we were smashed on a reef.

The engineer, who had been en route to Indonesia to work in the swamps, had brought boxes of condoms. Eventually we abandoned the boat and made a line to the shore - still in New South Wales. The following morning it was calm and the wreck was surrounded by condoms of various sizes - thus I was able to read in the Byron Bar newspaper: 'Pommy captain f***s boat." or words to that effect!

BACK TO CALMER WATERS

After returning to the UK, I took a job in Switzerland at Ecolé des Roches rather than taking a commission in the Royal Navy, and like so many of my colleagues, I taught English and skied three days per week. The school headmaster, known as the poisoned dwarf, was a rather demonic fellow who insisted on speaking French all the time, so I managed to miss most meetings during the first term and when I asked a bi-lingual student to sit at the front of the class and translate, I realised that my days there would be numbered.

Salvation came in the form of a summer language school at King's School, Wimborne in Dorset. The principal, Phil Duerdoth, had been to the same college as I had, St Luke's in Exeter, and needed an assistant. I was the man for the job.

Language schools in Britain in the mid-70s were far different than those of today; most were family-owned or run by slightly eccentric figures. To me the most notable among them was Dennis Monks, who used to transfer his students from Heathrow in a Rolls Royce and at the time of his British Council accreditation put his 84-year-old mother down as the homestay/welfare officer. When the British Council asked to interview her she was unable to get up the stairs to the school. Dennis also acted as an umpire for the Turkish Parrots cricket team, of which more later. He dressed in his striped cap and blazer, but sadly he knew few of the rules of cricket.

Bob Watts was and is another memorable figure in the UK language school industry. He formed close alliances with British Airways and was instrumental in initiating 'English in England' from Thailand, Central America, Japan, Korea and the Middle East. Bob needed somebody to travel to these far flung places. He had fond memories of his times in Australia and enjoyed the company of antipodeans. And so I became a marketing manager for the King's group of schools and subsequently for the British Tourist Authority.

My first trip to seek new students was with British Airways to Sudan - Khartoum to be precise. I had decided the format of my presentation as a brief introduction in both Arabic and English, a film, and then questions and answers. When I arrived in Khartoum I was told that the presentation was to be outside the British Council offices, in the desert. The projector was set up and I waited at the appointed house for people to arrive. Women to the left in purdah, men to the right, children left to roam. Four wheel drive vehicles were parked at the rear as were the camels. I started my presentation, a translation followed and it went well until we got half way through the film when a sandstorm blew up. The camels panicked, the projector was blown over, chaos ensued and mayhem erupted; camels and four-wheel drives seemingly drove everywhere. The British Council rep. in his pressed linen suit found me and told me that he could do with a stiff one, which in those days could have meant anything. I retired to the Hilton with the BA staff and insisted on buying them drinks. The hotel was one of the few places that served alcohol at that time and so they drank whisky chasers with a certain gusto. Those drinks cost more than my four nights' stay at the hotel.

SEEKING STUDENTS IN GUATEMALA

My next destination was Central America, visiting Panama, Costa Rica and Mexico among others. When I arrived in Salvador I hopped into a 'taxi' with no door or window handles. The driver asked me if I was an f***ing American gringo so I told him I was from New Zealand which totally perplexed him. It was the time of civil unrest in Salvador. Archbishop Romero had just been shot and as we slowed down for red traffic lights near Cathedral Square, a man came round the corner and opened fire with a machine gun. He caught the rear window which cascaded over me and left a few bullet marks in the car. I leapt onto the rear floor and the driver took off for the Sheraton like a man possessed.

The hotel only had six guests and we were each given two armed guards who followed us everywhere and we had a surreal evening in the bar. One of the strange things about travel is that your numbers are frequently swelled by one drunken German, as happened that night.

The armed guards came with me to the travel agency the following morning and stood at the ready outside the main door, much to the angst of the terrified staff. The British international schools were interested in attracting students, who had to travel by bus to Guatemala City airport and then fly to London. Guatemala at this stage was being run by a series of right wing dictators and genocide was prevalent amongst the Indian tribes. Yet Britain was a popular destination as most Central Americans were sick of being looked down upon by the Americans, even though many had become accountants in Miami. Charlie Safieh, BA's manager in Guatemala, and Suzy Clarke of Clarke Tours were characters of note during these troubled years.

Our agent in Mexico was Sergio Snyder, a celebrated classical pianist who lived with his partner, Roberto, a businessman of some repute. When I arrived his business colleague had just been murdered and he insisted on playing the role of a rather detached *mafioso* boss. He lived in elegant fashion and had no real interest in education except that it was a lucrative side line.

For me, Mexico is and always will be associated with Glyn Alban-Roberts, whose spending power within the British Tourist Authority is legendary. Whilst I was there, he entertained 150 people at the Winston Churchill restaurant at BTA expense, which consisted of 148 thespians, plus myself and a representative from British Airways. He did so much to promote the pink pound and tourism to Britain and the country is indebted to him as one of its most colourful appointees. Whilst he was in Mexico a major earthquake struck demolishing the BTA office. Glyn was supposed to be there and frantic calls were made, but to no avail. It transpired that Glyn was on a classical concert tour with Roberto and Sergio in Russia.

In his latter days at the BTA Glyn was asked to spend money in the last month of the fiscal year to ensure that it didn't go back into government coffers.

NEXT, PERU

It was late Thursday afternoon in Lima on my first visit to Peru. On arrival I had the stomach pangs and spent the night between the loo and the bed. I was there for an exhibition which started the following day at 9.00am. I left all my brochures on a table near the main entrance at 8.50am and took a hurried call. On returning all my literature had disappeared, grabbed by the invading horde, so I Sellotaped the only one that I had left in my bag and that had to do for the day.

Inexperienced, I'd allowed too much time to be there and had seen everyone who could possibly be of interest to me and me to them. Could I change my flight to Santiago from Monday afternoon to Saturday? No, there were no other flights!

The hotel in Lima feels as if it's under siege from the Shining Path guerrillas - there are armed guards around the building, the lobby is huge, ugly and depressing; the prospect of a weekend staying there, dispiriting. I wander around the giant lobby wondering what to do and, struggling with my very poor Spanish, read a notice on the travel agent's desk and eventually decipher it - they are promoting a trip to Macchu Picchu for the weekend. Departure, Saturday morning to Cusco, return flights, two nights' accommodation with breakfast, a half day tour of Cusco, an escorted return train journey to Machu Picchu and I'm interested. The price is also interesting. I inquire at the desk how much a night's accommodation is costing (the company) and when told, the decision is made. It costs less to take the tour for two nights than to stay in the hotel for one.

Early the next morning I'm collected and transferred to the airport, given tickets etc. and checked in, then proceeded to the departure gate where I see an elderly Boeing 707 operated by Fawcett Airlines. I recalled from years before that Michael Bentine was from Peru and his family were involved in the airline business and I worry - do I want to travel on an airline that thinks it's a piece of plumbing, with shareholders who are ex-Goons? The flight is called and habit propels me to the plane. Kindly, I think, I'm allocated a window seat and immerse myself in a book to take my mind off the possibilities of the plane's performance. It flies.

I read until my concentration is disturbed by announcements over the PA system and shouting from the passengers. Trying not to panic, I wonder what's happening and then understand; the in-flight entertainment is Housie, Housie (bingo) and the noise is other passengers shouting Casa, Casa and running down the aisle to collect their prizes - another flight on 'Plumbing Airlines'. We start to descend and I then wonder was the window seat such a kindly thought as at the end of the wing, through the cloud, I see a huge slab of rock - I look away and try to read my book and we land safely. The arrangements are surprisingly good. I'm met and put on a coach and taken to a charming old hotel where, before checking-in, I'm given a cup of something hot and unpleasant; a cure I'm assured for altitude sickness which I didn't know I had. The downside of flying to Cusco is the altitude, as Lima is on the coast, and a number of chums who have followed in my wake have suffered from altitude sickness... the locals combat it with coca leaves... which keeps you floating!

I'm told that the tour of Cusco will depart in an hour and I'm ready, but not for what I'm to see. The buildings, both ancient and old Spanish colonial, are stunning in their design, scale and execution and I feel slightly humble at the thought of what these people did so long ago with none of the modern tools and equipment that we now take for granted. We return to the hotel and are told to be ready at 0.500 the next day for the trip to Machu Picchu.

At a loose end, I decide to walk around the town to further examine some of the buildings. As I walk through the early evening quiet I become aware of an unidentifiable noise seemingly far away. I continue to walk and look and the noise becomes louder and I realise that it's discordant music. I follow my ears and emerge into the town square, which is heaving with Peruvian Indians clad in traditional and colourful dress. There are flags and banners and scattered through the crowds are groups of five or six musicians

21

playing with fierce and determined enthusiasm, not necessarily the same tune in the same group and definitely not the same as any other group. The noise is almost overwhelming and so is the curious smell.

I notice that much of the activity is centred on the impressive church built on the highest part of the square and push my way through the crowd. I see groups of men struggling out of the church, bearing huge and ornate triptychs that they parade through the cheering crowd and suddenly it dawns on me - I've arrived for the feast of Corpus Christi and how lucky I am. Or am I lucky? I realise that my feet are wet and also what the curious smell is - urine. The pavements and gutters are running with it as the frenetic musicians and Triptych carrying Indians just pass water wherever they are and whenever they need to. Eventually, I return to the hotel, remove and discard my socks and set about cleansing my shoes and that done, a meal and an early night.

The early morning call works and there are hot croissants and coffee available before I join the coach to the railway station. The train is modern, built in Spain and gleaming in the morning light. I'm escorted to my seat and find that I'm right at the front, almost beside the driver. He speaks little English and I speak little Spanish, but he explains as we draw out of the station that the railway was built by the British - I'm surprised.

He then explains, as we halt abruptly, that Cusco lies in a bowl surrounded by higher ground and that the train, to overcome this must go forward and back up a zigzag of railway lines to reach the top … and so we do. As we start our journey from the lip of the bowl, the sun illuminates the harsh panorama and again I think of the massive efforts of previous generations. I'm surprised to find that we follow a river for much of the time and the narrow gauge railway allows it to follow the tight contours of the route, so tight sometimes that it is easy to see the end of the relatively short train. There is evidence of past agricultural activity with abandoned terraces and irrigation schemes, but as we descend the land becomes more obviously fertile and eventually lush. The scenery is so alien to me that I scarcely notice the time passing, but I do notice the change in the geography with vast and abrupt hills rising out of the landscape. Late in the morning the train finally stops at an almost English-looking station beside the, by now, rapidly flowing and enlarged river at the foot of another enormous hill.

We disembark and board a very second-hand and high mileage Ford Transit minibus with a driver who appears to be about 11-years-old and who, with little thought for the passengers, launches the bus at the hill. I'm terrified as we lurch up the steeply zig-zagging track that has increasingly long drops off the side of it and whilst I should be taking in the tremendous views, I resort to closing my eyes and thinking what a coward I am.

The top is reached, my eyes open and the fear vanishes, replaced by awe. The aspect is stunning. I'm at the top of a 300 metre cliff and as far as the eye can see, in every direction, there is a carpet of impenetrable green forest, out of which rocky hills emerge and it seems quite incongruous to be standing beside a restaurant. I follow the signs and enter the ancient place that is Machu Picchu.

Often when travelling alone I had wished for company, but at this moment I needed none - I'm rendered speechless by the scale and the sense of history and puzzled by the events that led to its existence in the first place and its subsequent abandonment. I also think back to what it must have been like for Hiram Bingham when he discovered it in 1911 - he didn't know what he would find. At least I had some expectation, but that expectation was far exceeded by the reality. The remaining buildings were constructed of massive stones that fitted so closely together it was impossible to insert anything between them and of course I did try. How had they cut the stones so accurately and how had they manoeuvred them so precisely into position? There were no answers there and perhaps it was all the better to be confronted by the inexplicable.

All too soon the time came to go and reverse the process. Going downhill was no better than going up, but at least the size of the drops diminished as the journey progressed. The train was waiting and returned us on time, back to the hotel where I tried a local cocktail (or maybe more) which resulted in altitude sickness, or at least that's what I chose to think.

I was very lucky twice over - three days later the Shining Path guerillas attacked the train killing, or injuring most of the passengers in the coach I had occupied. Sometimes life seems to be all about timing!

ONWARDS TO ASIA

When I returned from Central America, I was pointed in the direction of Taiwan and Korea by the British Airways 'English in England' scheme. I was told that J.R. Lee would meet me in Seoul once I'd done a series of presentations in Taiwan with Jane Merrick from the Regent School. In both countries military service for young men was mandatory, so the market was extremely limited.

Jane and I were met in Taipei by one Albert Lee, a figure of some renown, who picked us up in a clapped out vehicle which rolled from side to side. He drove it at great speed which was highly unnerving as it had obviously been in numerous accidents. We stayed at the Lai Lai Sheraton, which in those days was the leading hotel in Taipei and attracted a large number of hookers in its bars. Every morning one would wake up to a number of pamphlets which had been poked under the door offering everything from personal services to heated toilet seats.

At this time, in 1979, very few people if any left Taiwan unless they were on organised tours, thus our presentations were exceedingly well attended. We had commitments in Taipei and Taichung and Albert insisted on driving us to the latter. Jane was three months' pregnant with her first child and as Albert dropped me off in Taichung a bus reversed into the Honda Civic in which we were travelling and Jane was still in the back seat. She refused to go any further and we both returned to Taipei smiling but in a state of high dudgeon.

Taipei was and is an unmissable city, you love it or hate it. Two years later I returned there with the first British Tourist Association sales mission to the Far East, led by Ivan Polunin and consisting of a number of leading figures in the service industry. On the way, we held presentations in Hong Kong before taking our flight to Taipei. We had no time for lunch and on arrival in Taipei were hosted by the government to exceedingly large gin and tonics followed by a dinner. Prior to the food, it is customary to toast everybody at the table, but here the tables were round and seated 18 people. Rice wine is quite potent on an empty stomach and after ten 'campai' toasts, people were beginning to falter, one participant passed out, another fell off his chair and everybody was filled with horror when the first course appeared, which was sea slug. I tried to talk while catching the slug with one hand and secreting it in my napkin; things soon became amusing with slugs flying everywhere.

Korea was my next stop. The chain smoking J.R. Lee met me and Sheila Barnes at Seoul airport. We were there to launch 'English in England' with British Airways. I was taken on a whistle stop tour of the universities and fed *bulgogli* at each stop. These are fatty strips of barbecue beef, plus cabbage with curry powder and garlic as a vegetable. It really does make you fart, in fact the whole nation farts. I soon learnt to avoid lifts as they resembled something out of a Peter Sellers film: "Who did it?"

At the end of the tour, a dinner was held in my honour with 18 professors from the universities and the inimical J.R. Lee. He had chosen a Mongolian restaurant with underfloor heating. We sat on cushions with our legs under a low slung table. I had to sit between two professors, one of whom was fascinated by British steam engines and the other was an expert on Thomas Hardy. Fortunately I was brought up in Dorset and went to school in Dorchester (Hardy's Casterbridge) but there is only so much one can say about *Tess of the D'Urbervilles* in limited English.

Just after the starter, I suffered incredible stomach pangs, something one never really gets used to. I took my leave from talking about steam trains and the Mayor of Casterbridge and rushed to the loo. There were footprints to stand in and a water spout half way up the wall. I flushed the loo but also soaked my trousers in the rush. On returning to the table the cushion on the floor had been removed and I sat on baking hot tiles. The professor who I had been talking to about trains wrongly thought that I was 'taking the michael' as I became shrouded in steam. Conversation ceased as the dinner came to an abrupt end, much to my embarrassment as people stared at this seeming apparition at the end of the table.

A similar thing happened in Colombia; I had made the fatal mistake of saying that I liked ethnic food in my early days of travel. I'd had a pretty long day after my taxi was pelted with stones by street urchins prior to arrival at the Tequendama hotel in Bogota. As I was waiting in the lobby, two American women were accosted outside and had their earrings ripped from their ears, an auspicious start to the day. One of our agents invited me for lunch and we went up to a restaurant overlooking the city. I got through the hot spicy starter but was hit by the pangs, so I made my excuses and retired. When I reappeared three hours later it was 4.30pm and they were clearing the restaurant and placing the chairs on the tables. My host was particularly unamused, especially when we were stopped on our return to the city and he was hauled away by the police because he didn't have his driving license with him or enough money to bribe the police. I was left on the side of the road with his partner to flag down a rather dodgy taxi.

THE SLEEPING GIANT

I have visited Indonesia - the Sleeping Giant - many times over the years, consistently failing to justify the time, money and effort expended, but always believing that I was on the verge of some sort of success. It never happened and I still wonder what I did wrong, or didn't do right. Even getting into Indonesia could be something of an adventure years ago - those days when you were still given a certificate by the airline confirming that you had crossed the equator and felt that you were something akin to an explorer.

On one occasion, I flew into Jakarta airport on a KLM flight from Amsterdam that involved several stops along the way and seeming to take forever to get there. Queuing in the inevitable long immigration line I found myself behind a pretty, if very fatigued, French woman who apart from the innumerable bags that many women seem to need, also had a babe in arms. Seeing her struggling I offered to help and for my trouble got the baby. This gave the mother the time to find her travel documents and to start completing the immigration form which she had been unable to do whilst on the flight. Written only in Bahasa Indonesian and English, I could see she was having difficulty in comprehending the way to fill it in and so offered advice. This was all very well until she came to the question: how many children are there travelling on your passport? She went completely white and I thought she was going to faint; she explained that she hadn't remembered to add the child to her passport. Her husband was awaiting her arrival and the child was on his passport and what could she do?

This was at a time when babies had been sold to childless couples and smuggled out of Indonesia and I could see that trying to go through and get her husband to get in touch with the immigration authorities etc. would be a problem. I had my own son on my passport and suggested she let me bring the child through, but she was worried because her child was female, but I reassured her that I had never seen immigration check the sex of a child. She didn't like it, but in the absence of any other solution she agreed, but this meant that she and I had to complete new immigration forms. Despite the encumbrance of the baby, I managed to complete my new form quicker than her and suggesting that it would be better if we went through separately, I went ahead and completed formalities with no problem.

Having been delayed, my case was available on the luggage carousel and so I automatically went on to customs, where for once I went through without a minute examination of everything. So there I was in Indonesia surrounded by the taxi drivers, porters and would-be tour guides with someone else's baby in my arms. I looked back and there was no sign of the woman. I looked around and couldn't see an obviously anxious father and so I stood wondering what to do, all the while fending off offers of taxis, hotels or help with my luggage. It was hot and the baby was clearly uncomfortable, but so was I and not just physically. Suppose the bay's mother had been refused entry, what would I do? I looked around and the crowd had thinned considerably and I still couldn't see a likely candidate as the father. I decided I would try going back to the customs area and as I did so I spotted the French woman and a man – relief!

I went towards them and it was obvious that some sort of Gaelic crises was in progress and I was standing there (still with the baby) whilst they continued. Eventually I managed to get their attention and I then became the focus of their displeasure, both of them apparently berating me in French. A KLM staff member came over and tried to help ease the situation, took the baby, thrust it into the mother's arms and said something which was sufficient to stop the bickering and they walked off - no goodbye and no thanks.

The charming KLM lady explained that the husband worked for a United Nations agency and consequently had a diplomatic passport that enabled him to enter the immigration area. He had been delayed in arriving at the airport and presumably as I came out, he went in. He found his wife (sans enfant) in near hysterics at the immigration desk as she had failed to complete her form properly and they weren't going to let her in. He was apparently furious with her for not putting the baby on her passport, for not filling in the form and for giving his child to a stranger - funny world sometimes. Freed from the encumbrance of someone else's child, I was ready to leave the airport and like taxis in London on a wet Friday evening, suddenly there were none. The lady from KLM was still lingering and seeing my problem offered me a lift into the city and at that moment I felt a very strong affection for the Dutch and quite the opposite for the French.

Part of this trip to Indonesia involved presentations in some of the lesser cities and my agent had telexed (pre-fax and e-mail days) with details of our itinerary, so I was prepared for the work to be done. What I wasn't prepared for were the vast distances involved, the entirely unreasonable flight times and the frequent intervening stops, but like anything, one can get used to it.
We had to go to Sulawesi and were to make a presentation in Ujung Pandang - I was really looking forward to going there, if only

because of the name. The flight took forever with frequent stops and delays, but eventually we arrived and were taken by a very mature taxi to the hotel - the sign claimed it was an Intercontinental, but I suspect that hotel chain knew nothing of it. We were made welcome and enjoyed a comfortable evening and reasonable food whilst discussing the following day's activities. My agent and I were to go to the local radio station in the morning to do an interview to back up the radio and press advertising, visit a local polytechnic at lunch time and I should then return to check the room was set up properly whilst he did some unspecified business.

The morning came and all things happened according to plan. Having checked the hotel meeting room, the sound system and projector, I decided that I would take a walk around the town before the evening presentation, so that at least I could offer comment when faced with the inevitable question - what do you think of...? I meandered down to the fishing wharf and watched others working, always a relaxing pastime, and walked back through the shopping area, looking quickly into what I took to be a museum, but turned out to be someone's home.

I made my way back towards the hotel and turned into the driveway that led to the entrance to be confronted by an armed soldier who appeared to prefer me not to go any further. I thought at first I'd made a mistake and turned into the wrong place, but no, Intercontinental hotel was clearly written on the building. I began to search my pockets for evidence that I was a guest and this was a thoughtless move, as it seemed to make the young soldier very agitated. I stopped, smiled and walked away thinking what to do.

My passport was with the hotel manager and my key was in reception. I had no identification other than a UK driving license and that was unlikely to impress. Perhaps the guard was only on the front gate and perhaps there was another way in? I started to walk, my hopes fading quickly as I realised there were soldiers posted every 50 metres, all armed and all looking bad tempered. I continued to walk right around the hotel and could see there was no way in. Where was my agent I wondered; inside or out? I walked around again and as the only obvious foreigner in the area the soldiers seemed to be taking a keen interest in my activities. It was getting dark and I was beginning to be seriously worried, but then I saw an officer walking out of the hotel drive, perhaps I could speak to him? As I tried a nonchalant approach the guards visibly stiffened, but I continued towards him, making sure my hands were clearly visible and wearing a probably inane smile on my face. The officer waved the guards away from me as I approached him and asked me in near perfect American English if he could help me.

I explained I was staying at the hotel and the guards wouldn't let me in and with that he called a guard over and got him to use his radio to check my claim and, finding it was true, walked me back to reception. We chatted as we walked and he was interested to know why I was in Ujung Pandang and I explained about the presentation on 'English in England' that I was to do that night and invited him to come and see.

He looked suddenly sad and moving away from the hearing of others explained to me that an un-named general, an important figure both politically and militarily, had decided to stay at the hotel for the night and his security was vital, so much so that no one save *bone fide* guests would be allowed on the premises. I asked him about those wishing to attend the presentation and he said simply that there would be no presentation. With restraint I pointed out the investment and effort that had been made and he shrugged. At this point my agent, Mr Phillipus, appeared in the distance, also being prevented from entering the hotel, and I asked the officer if he could arrange to let him in and it was done. But Mr Phillipus was not easily placated and set to making his position very clear - an impressive performance from a small man confronted by armed soldiers. When he finally ran out of time the officer spoke few words, but enough, apparently - they both shrugged and that was that, although as an afterthought Mr Phillipus did talk to the authorities, again warning them there might be a crowd trying to get in to the hotel that night. Certainly large numbers of people did try to get in, but we couldn't find out if they were coming for the presentation or for other purposes.

Mr Phillipus and I were the only diners in the restaurant that night, but towards the end of the evening we were invited to join the military party and we did, accepting their hospitality with as good grace as possible. We left the next morning to fly back to Jakarta. There was no hotel bill and a car had been provided by the military to take us to the airport where we went directly to the plane without bothering to check-in - small recompense.

Departing from Jakarta could be just as bad as arriving. On checking in one was automatically told that there was no record of a reservation and once that matter had been sorted out one's luggage was always overweight; they had very special scales in Jakarta in those days. A small amount of money tucked in with the ticket was always the way to 'confirm' a reservation, but I finally decided that the overweight charge was too much. I waited until the last moment to check-in and went through the performance, first with the lack of and then mysterious appearance of a confirmed seat. I was then subjected to the overweight treatment and said I couldn't afford excess baggage. Their faces dropped and they went into a huddle. Half the amount was suggested. I said I had nothing and perhaps the easy way out of the problem was if they brought me a rubbish bin.
"What for?"
"Well, I have lots of unimportant papers in my suitcase and I'll just take them out and throw them away - it shouldn't take more than half an hour to complete."

32

My bag went through immediately and even appeared at my destination.

THE RIVER KWAI

My early memories of Thailand are collecting suits from the tailor at the Old Erawan Hotel, now demolished, for Bob Watts my boss and meeting Pravit who was the British Airways sales manager in Bangkok. He was educated at Wellington and retained a passion for rugby throughout his life. His home had the most amazing selection of phallic symbols and I always remember him meeting me at the airport in a T-shirt with an exceedingly large penis on the front. He eventually retired from BA having been instrumental in setting up 'English in England' in the Thai summer holidays (March-May). At one stage, up to 420 students were coming to spend up to six weeks in a consortia of schools, the majority going to KSE. I held a yearly presentation in February each year and these were extremely well attended.

I love Bangkok and not for the commonly thought reasons. I love it because it's noisy, dirty, smelly, polluted, congested and the people are unremittingly cheerful and polite. But even though I love the city, the opportunity for a trip outside is something to take with alacrity when my favourite agent and good friend suggested an excursion to the River Kwai. This was in the days before the new road network had been built. However, we eventually got clear of the city and headed for Kanchanaburi, 130km to the north west.

After a number of trips to Asia and to Thailand in particular, we had learned about Asian planning so refrained from asking for details about the trip, knowing full well that plans are not finalised until whatever is being planned has actually occurred. There was an excursion to yet another magnificent wat (temple), several attempted stops to find a toilet that was considered satisfactory for foreigners to use and one for refreshment where, to our consternation, a live bear was ambling around the restaurant.

We passed the famous 'Bridge Over the River Kwai' but didn't stop as we were inevitably running late and the light was beginning to fade; a familiar problem we're told. Eventually we reached a settlement beside the river where a number of longtail boats are drawn up on the bank. Longtail boats held a fascination for me from the first time I ever visited Thailand. These long, narrow and fairly flimsy vessels are powered by car engines varying in size and power, but could be V8s. Mounted on a crudely welded 'Y' bracket and fitted with a 5-7m prop shaft they were treated just as we would a conventional outboard motor.

Prolonged negotiations took place, all the while the tropical evening light fading away and finally just before dark we're told to board the selected boat. We nose out into the muddy and quite fast flowing river and head upstream. There is an old, old man on the helm and a young boy in the prow and the young one is obviously the eyes for the old. We see from time to time, large rocks sticking out of the water and as it darkens further we see them only as we veer away from them. We are concerned as our good friend tells us there are crocodiles and lapses into peals of laughter. We don't know if she's joking, or practicing Buddhist pragmatism.

After about 40 minutes (although it seemed much longer at the time) the boat slows as we see a chain of lights reflecting in a backwater of the river and as we approach, we discover that there is a row of bamboo rafts moored there and we hear the steady throb of a generator. Voices call out in a language we don't recognise and very quickly we're moored alongside and there are people helping us out and our bags vanish. Reception is on one raft together with part of the bar and restaurant and we smell the unfamiliar odour of French cooking. The formalities are completed quickly and we are

34

escorted across rickety footways between the rafts to a simple and clean bamboo room compete with an en suite bathroom. Dinner as soon as we are ready, we're told. A refreshing cold shower and we return to the dining raft. Cold beer is produced from a net hanging in the river and we're told dinner will be served shortly.

We find out that the rafts are operated by a French man and his Thai wife - he cooks the evening meal (no choice) and she does lunch (again no choice) and this suits us perfectly - four weeks of staying in hotels and having to choose from a menu does begin to pall and it's lovely to have someone else make the decision. The meal is excellent and so is the wine produced as if by magic by our friend Lek. We sit in the soft light of the oil lamps, the generator having been switched off, listening to the sounds of the invisible jungle and the barely visible river and it seems we are very close to paradise.

A deep and undisturbed sleep allows us to wake at first light and see where we are. We're about 20m off shore and surrounded by quite steep hills covered in a jungle of bamboo and unidentifiable trees. Through the jungle we can see there are footpaths and occasionally we catch a glimpse of some sort of wildlife and can hear in the distance the sound of falling water. There are fish jumping in the river and fishermen trying to catch them and we see a quite large barge proceeding slowly upstream, carrying we know not what.

We carefully make our way to the eating raft - the passage of the barge has set the rafts bobbing on the water - and we are greeted by the immaculate Frenchman. Fresh croissants have been prepared, the coffee smells authentic and Sue completes perfection by producing her travelling pot of Marmite. Lek joins us and starts to tell us the plan, but is side tracked by the Frenchman, although this does reveal more about the situation. We discover that the reason we didn't understand the language spoken by the staff was that they were all from Burma (as it was then) and members of one of the tribes being persecuted by the military regime. The Mon people seem to be so gentle and kind we cannot imagine anyone persecuting them.

Breakfast over, we go ashore but don't know why. I'm given a large and quite heavy bag to carry and the two ladies stride-off purposefully into the jungle. I follow. We climb through the lush vegetation and the day warms as we move into the sun and suddenly I realise that the jungle has been tamed - I'm walking under a man-made banana leaf walkway and at the end of this there is a village. It is very neat and tidy and Sue and Lek are surrounded by a group of uniformed children on their way to school. The teacher comes to get the children away and starts talking to Lek and I know from the glances and hand gestures, I'm being volunteered for something and I'm right, finding myself giving an impromptu English lesson to 45 children aged six to 11.

On one occasion I arrived in Thailand to be told at the airport that there was a BA area managers' lunch and I was cordially invited. The meal was held at a Chinese/Thai restaurant and we sat around a circular table. I had just arrived from the wintry January chill of the UK and the local temperature was 34 degrees plus, with an air conditioning system in the restaurant which was on the blink and I began to sweat profusely. In the early days I was not too proficient with chopsticks and every time the table whizzed around I seemed to end up with a trail of food to my dish which was incredibly embarrassing as I was the guest of honour.

Damon Mullaney was leaving his post as BA manager and he invited us all out for a night at his favourite salubrious hotspots and we would be offered a BA discount for any services offered. We all ended up on marble slabs covered in lather by the ladies of the night. It was a walk on the seedy side especially at the Kangaroo club which had a live sex show. Bangkok in the 70's and early 80's was a vibrant city with great charm and one never felt threatened. Sex was, and is, an industry and the place thrives on it but tries to pretend that it just doesn't happen. With the onset of Aids and STDs most foreigners are far more wary but the vacuum has been filled by Indians, Arabs and Pakistanis who fly in on charters especially to Pattaya for one thing only. Thailand is the Land of Smiles and to a degree corruption, in our terms, is endemic. Votes are bought at elections either with the offer of cash or mobile phones or new roads /electricity for the community.

National Service in the army is compulsory if your birth date comes up and young men have to serve 18 months. After three months compulsory training one group of young men were lined up on the parade ground and told by the commanding officer that they had two choices: either hand over their debit cards and PIN numbers and walk through the gates or stay and complete the next 15 months... there must be some wealthy army officers methinks.

The Thai attitude to sex, as with corruption, is somewhat ambivalent. I also had visions of watching the Katoi regiment... the girlie-boys prancing in high heels and make up. It must be quite a sight.

A HOTEL FIRE IN HONG KONG

The diversity and energy are the first things to hit any traveller in Hong Kong, as well as the Orwellian impression of the old international airport. The hustle and bustle are endemic and one can't help but be carried in the sway. Sadly the 'old' feel of the place has disappeared and the tower blocks seem to dominate the skyline. Everybody has to dress in the latest fashion and possess the latest gadgets, to have is to be, to show and to wear is all important. One is left wondering what lies beneath? There is a genuine concern to educate one's offspring. But education seems to be totally allied with future financial gain rather than the broader aspects of learning.

I feel very much as though I'm in a goldfish bowl, slightly surreal and overpowered by the masses and seemingly eccentric expats who find the opportunity to expose their views on the lost colonies or the skinhead Leeds supporters who manage to pursue their tribal instincts. Chinese culture has given us so much in the West and yet it seems to be losing itself in a mass of consumerism and greed.

It was a chilly night by Hong Kong standards and, as always, difficult to sleep with the constant traffic noise and babble of people's chatter. I had been moved earlier that day from a rather salubrious suite on the 12th floor to a room on the seventh floor. I slept fitfully as I had spent the evening eaten drunken prawns and drinking vast amounts of alcohol with the BTA rep. and was awakened by a phone call from the UK at 0.100am regarding a business meeting. At 0.40am I was roused again by the sound of regimented Chinese shouts and crashing and thought that the hotel must be next to a martial arts school. I dozed and heard people in the corridors. I staggered out of bed to the window to be faced by a fireman about to smash my window. With glass and a chair hurtling to the ground I caught sight of two people on a ledge and the air conditioner was pumping putrid smoke into the room. The Chinese are certainly not renowned for their humour. One couldn't open any of the windows in the room, they were all locked - sometimes you have to laugh... it must be a dream. There was no fire-bell, nobody had knocked on the door - I thought 'Oh shit...*Towering Inferno*' - stick a towel over your head. By the time I had reacted, the window was smashed, water was spraying everything, the fireman spoke to me in totally unintelligible English and I realised what a language barrier really means in a so-called English-speaking country. I grabbed a bag, shot out the door and down the stairs. There was total mayhem amongst the people and children, and I was one of the last to leave the hotel, sprayed by the glass on the pavement.

The overall organisation was appalling. A major tragedy could have occurred. One is always at risk in moderately priced hotels but it is only a matter of time before:

14 in hospital after fire in Hongkong hotel

HONGKONG, Thurs. — Fire broke out in a hotel today, putting 14 people in hospital, and police classified the blaze as arson.

A police spokesman said an arson team was probing the pre-dawn blaze at the 221-room Imperial Hotel, where more than 300 guests and staff were evacuated.

Hospital officials said five people had been discharged by late today while the other nine were in fair condition.

The injured included Australians, Americans, a Filipina, and a Korean.

A hotel official told re-porters the fire started on the 12th floor of the building in Hongkong's Tsimshatsui tourist district at 4.45 am.

"We called the fire department when we could not control the fire," the official said.

Canadian teacher Jean Eccles, evacuated to safety from the 16th floor, said she was awakened by banging sounds.

"I thought, my goodness, they start construction early around here. I was about to complain to the manager when I found out they were trying to warn guests," she said. — Reuter.

FIREMEN had to resort to extension ladders to rescue trapped guests during the fire last night.

AN injured tourist being taken to an ambulance.

Imperial Hotel fire: it's arson, say cops

POLICE are classifying the fire that broke out in the Imperial Hotel yesterday as a case of arson. A police spokesman said no one has been detained as yet and investigations into the motive of the crime are being handled by a special team comprising police and fire officers.

Police believe the culprit or culprits may have used petrol in the fire which began near the lift on the 12th floor of the 19-storey hotel in Tsim Sha Tsui.

Yesterday afternoon, a party of government chemists were sent to the hotel to look for evidence.

Fourteen people, all tourists, were hurt in the fire, and nine of them were still in hospital last night. Eight were in fair condition while the condition of the ninth is satisfactory.

The fire, which started at dawn, was put out within an hour. The hotel, which has 221 rooms, was almost fully occupied, and

—by—
Henry Leung

most of the 300 guests were asleep when the fire started.

Thirteen fire engines and 80 firemen were deployed to fight the fire. Firemen, several of whom wore breathing apparatuses, used extension ladders to rescue guests who were trapped on the upper floors.

A fire officer said the thick smoke from the fire had impeded attempts by the guests to find their way out from the upper floors.

Several guests broke the glass windows of their rooms with furniture to draw the firemen's attention.

On one occasion, firemen fought their way up to the floor which had caught fire only to find hotel guests rushing down the same staircases.

About 70 guests were led to safety. Some of them suffered from cuts, while others were overcome by smoke.

● WITNESSES' accounts and more pictures on Page 3

A DAZED hotel guest with cuts on his hands being helped to safety.

THE BIRTHDAY!

Travel may broaden the mind, but it can also be confusing, particularly when it's been a long trip and involved other cultures and Hong Kong can be confusing, even if you live there and for the brief visitor it can be more so. Perhaps it was this confusion which affected my good friend Norman Harris. Crossing between Hong Kong and Kowloon on the wonderful Star Ferry and reading his notes for the next meeting and juggling a map at the same time, he was suddenly struck by the date - October 29, his wife's birthday! He had been married 15 years and at last had been able to remember the date un-prompted, but since it was already the actual day, a degree of panic set in. The force may not have been with us, but at least the time change was. It was still only 17.00 in the UK, so we set off to find a phone and directory inquiries for the number of the florist in our home town, who fortunately was a friend. Norman was connected to make his plea for help, and then came relief as he was assured that a bouquet would be delivered within the hour. That done, it was back to work.

While relating the matter of 'other cultures' I cannot resist including here a souvenir from Beijing sent to me by a friend. It is from a hotel brochure for guests, translated by the management from the original Mandarin:

Getting There
Our representative will make you wait at the airport. The bus to the hotel runs along the lake shore. Soon you will feel pleasure in passing water. You will know that you are getting near the hotel, because you will go round the bend. The manager will await you in the entrance hall. He always tries to have intercourse with all new guests.

The Hotel
This is a family hotel, so children are very welcome. We of course are always pleased to accept adultery. Highly skilled nurses are available in the evenings to put down your children. Guests are invited to conjugate in the bar and expose themselves to others. But please note that ladies are not allowed to have babies in the bar. We organize social games, so no guest is ever left alone to play with them self.

The Restaurant
Our menus have been carefully chosen to be ordinary and unexciting. At dinner, our quartet will circulate from table to table, and fiddle with you.

Your Room
Every room has excellent facilities for your private parts. In winter, every room is on heat. Each room has a balcony offering views of outstanding obscenity! You will not be disturbed by traffic noise, since the road between the hotel and the lake is used only by pederasts.

Bed
Your bed has been made in accordance with local tradition. If you have any other ideas please ring for the chambermaid. Please take advantage of her. She will be very pleased to squash your shirts, blouses and underwear. If asked, she will also squeeze your trousers.

Above All
When you leave us at the end of your holiday, you will have no hope. You will struggle to forget it.

'DRUNKEN SHRIMPS' AND KIM CHI

On to Taipei next for a brief stop to make an afternoon presentation after which to find myself invited to a celebration. I was collected from the hotel and taken to another where we went to an enormous banqueting hall seething with people and I note that I'm the only non-Chinese. However I'm made to feel welcome and escorted to what seems a suspiciously conspicuous table. Bottles of Cognac are on the table, which the Taiwanese are rapidly getting outside of, and I cautiously inquire if a beer is a possibility. Certainly! A crate is placed beside me.

The banquet starts and all's well at first. I manage to use the chopsticks without really disgracing myself and as each new dish arrives I take some until I'm confronted with a dish on which the meal is moving. I raise an eyebrow to my companion and he explains it's a very special dish and roughly translated as 'drunken shrimps'. The fresh shrimps have been put on the dish and then covered in rice wine. The trick is to wait until they've almost stopped moving due to their drunken stupor and then eat them, allowing them to rest on the tongue before swallowing! I'm not at all keen, but I sense the eyes of the world are upon me, so have no choice. Perhaps the beer helped, but actually, it wasn't the worst culinary experience I ever had; what was worse was that no one told me there were 26 courses and I hadn't paced myself for this. By the end of the night I was bursting and the next day when I checked in at the airport I thought the airline would charge me excess weight on my body.

And so to Korea, still at that time something of an unknown entity and as far as I was concerned, aptly named 'the Hermit Kingdom' but in fairness, each time it had got better and on this visit I was taken care of by an excellent agent – Mr W. K. Kim. I was there for several days and was entertained handsomely, eating mostly local dishes, which I was beginning to like. Foolishly it seems with the clarity of hindsight, I expressed considerable enthusiasm for a local delicacy *kim chi*, a peculiar mixture of cabbage, garlic vinegar, garlic, chilies and more garlic, which had been induced to ferment, producing a very memorable condiment.

At the end of what subsequently could be seen to have been a very successful trip, I departed for home, leaving directly from my Seoul hotel for Kimpo airport on their shuttle bus, rather than drag my agent all the way there through the congestion of the city. As I stepped from the bus, there he was together with his wife who had taken the trouble to dress in traditional costume to bid me farewell - a lovely gesture. Mr Kim had some influence at the airport and my check-in was accomplished with no delay and we went for coffee before I went through to departure.

As I turned to leave having said goodbye, Mrs Kim proffered a cloth-covered object - a parting gift. Inside was a clay pot, not an item of great beauty but clearly significant. She, speaking no English, turned to her husband who explained it was a pot of her own homemade *kim chi* that she had buried in the garden for five months - something to really appreciate.

THE MIDDLE EAST EXPERIENCE

During the early '80s there was a great demand for language education from the Middle East. Schools in Britain had traditionally been flooded with large groups from Iran, Libya, Japan, etc. and now it was the era of the Arabs.

In 1980, we had 140 students from IAL, Saudi Arabia, who were going to train as air traffic controllers. When they first arrived they decided to use the car park as a prayer area, which wasn't great for people trying to get to and from work. They had arrived at the weekend and by the first Tuesday there were a large number of calls from host families complaining that their toilet seats had been broken and their bathrooms flooded. It transpired that the students had been squatting on the toilet seats and flooding the bathrooms in order to wash their feet before prayers. Thus began my first lesson in teaching Arab students how to crap! It came back to haunt me many years later as I squatted in the *majlis* on the floor, having to sit on my left hand so that I didn't use it to eat food as I am naturally left handed and that hand has only one use in Arab culture.

The Middle East was a cultural experience second to none as I sat at an exhibition faced by a Saudi with his wife standing three paces behind in complete purdah, covered from head to toe. He had no English, but she did, so every question was asked and answered by her. Women were not allowed to drive and had to cover themselves, but one still saw Air France hostesses in bra-less T-shirts in the souks. On my first trip I was in the souk just before evening prayers when the religious police came around with their knobbed sticks and belted anybody still trading. I met one dejected Englishman in a hotel lobby who had come from Blackpool with samples of Blackpool rock, only to find that in the intense heat they had all melted and turned to glue.

I am often reminded of the time when the American pilot told his passengers, to 'turn your clocks back 500 years, you are now entering the Kingdom of Saudi Arabia'.

In the mid-eighties I took an educational sales mission to Riyadh and Jeddah. It transpired that a number of the brochures taken there for various schools and tourist boards had churches on them, so they were immediately confiscated by customs. Then brochures which had women's arms and legs showing were also taken, to be returned, when they did come back at all, with the offending limbs having been coloured in at the local primary school, as were the international papers with any offending advertisements showing women with bare heads.

On a later trip, the Scottish Tourist Board had all their brochures confiscated as whisky distilleries were shown; but men in kilts were acceptable - incredible hypocrisy, apparently because of Saudi's oil wealth. I once took a group of leading Saudi travel agents on a trip to the Lake District and Scotland. A colleague had already spent two days in Blackpool with them and I met the group on Lake Windermere at a very upmarket hotel. After dinner they asked if I could arrange some company for them as they were all males. I told them that it was not in my brief but to speak to the concierge. He duly phoned various parlours and within two hours a group of ladies of the night arrived on a chartered bus, no expense spared, from Penrith to Carlisle. The rougher the better it seemed... activities soon deteriorated and members of the group had to be asked to leave the foyer and continue their activities elsewhere in the hotel. The following morning the hotel resembled a war zone with articles of clothing strewn throughout the place. We left thereafter for a day with the 'Romantic poets'!

THE POSTPONED WEDDING

In the latter part of 1986, my mother sadly died in New Zealand on the Thursday before I was due to marry on Saturday September 26 and we had to postpone our wedding celebrations. Many of my chums thought that I had got cold feet because, aged 39, this was my first time around, so instead of heading off on safari in Kenya we travelled to a funeral in a wet and windy Nelson 6,000 miles away. We had to pay full fares on Qantas as we were so late in booking and could only get separate seats. The Aussie lady next to me wouldn't move nor would the person next to my bride, Woodsie,

46

so I had no option but to stand up and make an impassioned plea to my fellow passengers. We were inundated with offers as well as champagne throughout the flight.

We flew into Nelson and my sister Jilly had kindly arranged everything but we were met with: "Would you like to see Mother?" I had visions of her appearing, but she'd been kept in a coffin in the hall for a funeral on the Monday.

Thereafter we drove down the West Coast to Christchurch to stay with Wendy De La Bere, a lady who has had a major influence in my life. She was a true thespian who had a passionate interest in Shakespeare and was instrumental with Yvette Bromley and others in establishing the Court Theatre in Christchurch which still thrives today. I had co-produced two plays with her and had very minor acting parts in others. She was always slightly eccentric with a love of Italy and a heart of gold. In her later years she wore empty pill packets in the shape of a cross around her neck and had a flamboyant sense of dress, happiest when driving in her convertible and going fishing. She introduced me to Anglo-Catholicism at St Michael's and acted as a surrogate mother during my early years in New Zealand.

Once back in UK, we rearranged our wedding blessing for November so that we could have a joyous occasion. The only problem was that I had planned on being with the Scottish polo team and would be cutting it fine to make the day. Sod's law, my flight was delayed on the way back and I arrived on the Saturday morning with the blessing in the afternoon. It was a memorable day, Te Ariki Rampata Hatherly acted as master of ceremonies and Norman Harris was best man.

PRINCE CHARLES AND 'MY TAILOR'!

After the wedding, we took off for the Welsh hills for just a couple of days as I was due to be in Jeddah on the Wednesday. I was involved with the British Week activities there, which Prince Charles and Princess Diana were scheduled to open. But when I dashed off to the airport for my flight to Jeddah I mistakenly picked up the suitcase with our dirty laundry from our few days away and arrived at my hotel in Saudi with only the T-shirt and jeans I was wearing. I rang home in a fraught state asking to ask Woodsie to send out the correct suitcase. I was supposed to be meeting the great and the good that morning at 11 o'clock at the High Commission.

The concierge told me that the only place to get clothes early in the morning was at the souk where there was a Pakistani tailor who opened early. I headed there at first light only to find that the one suit he had in my size was purple with wide lapels and bell bottom trousers. The shirt didn't fit and all of this was offset by a tie which was wide and a dreadful colour, and a pair of black plastic shoes... a sight to behold!

I turned up at the High Commission and was met at the door by a chap who was obviously ex-Guards and Eton and his county set wife, Priscilla. Everybody glared at me. We were lined up to meet the Royals and I was placed at the end, one step back. When Prince Charles came round he shook my hand warmly and said: "I do like your tailor." I replied: "I couldn't possibly recommend him."

The following day my suitcase arrived and I was appropriately suited and booted. At the opening of the exhibition HRH caught me out of the corner of his eye and came over with the opening gambit: "I'm so pleased to see that you've changed your tailor." He was hurried away as Idi Amin began to lurk in the hall.

The following day was TAIF day, 'thank Allah it's Friday'. Because the High Commission was able to serve alcohol it became an incredibly popular place. According to local folklore, one former ambassador, who was in Saudi to dry out, received a call from the airport on one occasion to be told that his grand piano, which had just arrived, was leaking... whisky galore!

CONFLICT IN IRAN

I was staying in Dubai when I received a telex from Bob Watts, the owner of King's School, asking me to go onto Teheran as an agent there was proving difficult to contact and owed £250,000 which was a huge amount of dosh in the late '70s. The only flight into Tehran was from Kuwait and it was the last flight in, due to the fighting at the airport and the conflict with the Shah. The flight was full of fleeing mullahs, women in *niqabs* and two drunken Germans.

When we landed at the airport the local militias loyal to Khomeini were fighting for control of the airport with troops loyal to the Shah. As we taxied into the airport we could see the shattered glass from the airport buildings and it brought back images from earlier in the day on CNN when I had seen shattered images of the front of the Intercontinental hotel where I was supposed to be staying. I was met at the bottom of the aircraft stairs by a BA hostess who told me that due to the demise of the hotel I would travel into town in the crew minibus and would be staying with Chris Cross, the BA manager. The minibus would drop me at his office.

As we drove into town along Liberation Avenue (formerly Shah Reza Avenue) young men were hiring automatic rifles for passers-by to take pot shots at pictures of the Shah hanging on trees. It would have been so easy to turn and fire on the minibus.

49

I was dropped at the BA office which had already been vandalised by the local militia and everything in it had been broken, destroyed or ripped. Amidst all this mayhem sat Chris Cross in a pinstripe suit and bow tie, holding a meeting with a local business contact - the epitome of an Englishman, the stiff upper lip. When he'd finished he said that the hotel was too dangerous to stay in and that I was welcome to stay in his apartment as his family had returned to the UK. I was to be very wary as the local militias could raid the flat at any time and it was a case of mum's the word. I was nearly wetting myself. On arrival at the apartment he told me to settle in and come to the lounge at 7.45pm as 'the fun' started at 8pm. I did as I was told and we re-arranged all the furniture, angling the sofas and chairs, but I was baffled by his comments. At 7.55pm an American from Bell helicopters appeared who had been hidden in the attic. It was certainly a dangerous time for any American.

We had a couple of stiff drinks and then the show started in the northern suburbs. There was machine gun fire, bazookas and rockets. Apparently, 'the fun' started at 8pm every night. I guess the forces of the Shah and the militias had to get home from work and eat before attacking one another.

I tried to trace the agent who owed the money but he had disappeared into the Evrin jail. I was on a futile exercise, scared witless. The airport was closed to outgoing flights as the control tower had been destroyed and Chris was bringing in some flights by radio/walkie-talkie. I was holed up in his flat for five days and rapidly became quite gung-ho about the adventure.

Then Chris said that there was an Olympic Airways flight leaving for Athens and he could possibly get me onto it, so we headed to the airport. I remember carrying carpets through the security as he escorted me to the plane. It was full so I ended up with the carpets in the loo, but with a plentiful supply of drinks and managed to get rather the worse for wear... *quelle* relief.

I sent Bob a telex from Athens telling him that trying to get money in Tehran was like a punk rocker trying to get into Buckingham Palace and that I was taking a holiday in Greece. He was not a happy chappie.

The only other time that I have travelled in the toilet of a plane was in Kota Kinabalu, on the coast of Borneo. The wife of the British Council representative there asked me if I would like to visit some of the tribes that lived in the jungle as she operated a mobile library service. We travelled in a clapped out army truck and drank the local hotchpotch in palm leaves. When I got to the airport, which in those days was a tin shack in the middle of nowhere, the loo was closed. It was 38 degrees and sweltering. I walked across the tarmac in the scorching tropical sun, sweating profusely, when I was hit by the stomach pangs. I couldn't turn back so ended up like Charlie Chaplin shuffling to the aircraft. Once on board I headed straight to the loo and wouldn't come out until we landed in Singapore, much to the consternation of the crew. Sometimes a man has to do what a man has to do!

And once in Mexico, I was struck down by 'Montezuma's revenge' at the airport and was so ill that the flight ended up leaving without me and the challenge then was to get out of the 'no man's land' of the airport terminal and get another flight; not an easy task by any stretch of the imagination.

AND SO TO AFRICA…

I arrived in Dakar relaxed, having had the by now traditional Bloody Mary on the flight. Feeling fortified, I went to the baggage lounge to be met by a man with a Novotel/Meridien badge on his white coat. I thought - marvellous what service, until he pushed my bags to the rear exit door and his accomplice pulled up in a clapped-out Peugeot.

He got in as well and I thought... Oh dear! We'd gone about two miles when the question of money arose and I thought, keep talking. I had visions of being left by the side of the road. The car broke down twice and they got pretty heavy but somehow the show stayed on the road. On arriving at the approach to the hotel the car stopped and I got my bags out, relieved. One of the two men was very tall and the other short and slight. He haggled over the fare - they wanted 20,000 CFA, whereas the normal fare was 6,000 CFA. I gave them 3,000 each and could sense things were about to turn nasty. The little guy was going to grab me so I knee'd him in the crotch and swung a right upper cut on the tall guy, catching him fair and square. The guard from the hotel came over, saw what had happened, said nothing and escorted me to the hotel.

I was heading to Banjul and a good friend, David Stubbings, had advised me to catch the bus from Dakar to Banjul as it was air-conditioned. They spoke English and it was an interesting way to see the countryside. I boarded it at 11am. There were three passengers and an English speaking conductor - what luxury. At 11.30am we pulled round a corner and the bus filled up. I felt slightly conspicuous in a 'safari' suit with matching briefcase and suitcase and other passengers ignored the seat next to me. Eventually a woman got on with four chickens in a box and sat down. She was friendly, colourful and smiled a lot, but the chickens stank. About 5km out of Dakar, one of them started to crap. It was like a bad holiday in Egypt. The excrement went down the side of the box onto my trousers and briefcase. I started off with *'votre poulet merde'*, 'your chicken is shitting'. Still a blank look. Then sign language, which she thought was hilarious, as did everybody else on the bus. I would have done as well - if I hadn't been wedged there for six and a half hours and I was high.

The next stage was a river crossing and we eventually got off at the ferry terminal in Banjul and waited in the cattle yard for this wreck of a boat to appear; one had sunk the previous year in calm water. I was the only white man, laden with bags and smelling foul. Four Africans got on with a dead pig with its stomach gutted and headed straight for me, plonking the pig next to me. The boat was crowded, I couldn't move.

On arriving at the Atlantic hotel, people backed away from me. I rang the laundry: "So sorry sir, no porter service on a weekend." *C'est la vie.*

CAMEROON – A DAY AMONGST 'EM

It was Douala and I woke up from a light sleep, having visited the loo on a number of occasions. Not that I have anything against crocodile steaks and baboon legs but my stomach does. I had spent the evening at one of those interminable cocktail parties surrounded by our black brothers in ill-fitting suits talking about the wonders of Britain through a haze of body odour, and old Africa hands who thought they were still in the colonies and yelling loudly for 'the boy'. At the end of the evening, as I walked outside the hotel, a number of female workers approached from the bushes making it quite obvious how much they charged for a variety of services.

So I woke up feeling like a dead monkey only to find the water was off. This presents problems for someone with a dodgy stomach. There was no coffee or tea in the hotel and no likelihood of any for 12 hours. My room stank, I stank and had a meeting with the minister of information in an hour. I just had to go.

It's strange to be sitting in a taxi smelling yourself in 90 degree humidity and praying as you make spasmodic farts. The minister was extremely pleasant and he knew Bradford; but his secretary left me speechless, she was both off-hand and up herself, it must be the influence of living in a French colony. I don't know what upset her, as I hadn't been shouting that loud. The local TV station was now operational but not showing programmes as they couldn't afford to make or buy any. I offered them three: 1. Life on the Underground. 2. Holidays in Brixton. 3. Scottish Castles.

I made the usual circuit of the embassy, the British Council and the travel trade office before returning to the hotel. There was only one choice... a swim. Unfortunately, the pool was covered in flotsam from a lot of dirty guests... still what the hell! I dirtied up then went back to my room only to be faced by a flood - all my belonging were awash on the floor as the maid had left the taps on.

I rushed to the airport late - only to have the taxi driver pick up seven kids at different schools on the way and I paid for the bloody taxi. On arrival at the airport the heavens opened, the plane was delayed for over four hours and the lights went out as the electricity failed five times. In the end, I waited seven hours until we eventually took off in a 30-seater through the most horrific storm I've ever seen.

FOLLOW THAT...

I really thought I'd reached the pits - until I visited Liberia. It was a hot dusky afternoon as the plane taxied into the decrepit airport building, the queues were horrendously long through immigration and the hallways stank of human pee. Though my passport and visa were in order, the latter was not signed correctly - $10; the first official had stamped the wrong part of the visa - $10; suitcase passed customs - $10. Having got through penniless I then discovered that the airport was 40 kilometres from the town. Fortunately I'd been talking to a Frenchman who offered me a lift with his driver. Monrovia must be one of the few African airports where you're not swarmed upon by hordes of boys trying to grab your bags. I guess because it's so far from anywhere.

Five kilometres from the airport we were stopped at a road check - $5... another ten kilometres - $5... and so on into town. It transpired that none of the government workers had been paid since the previous October, so the easiest ways for soldiers and police to make money was stopping cars. I assured Henri, the Frenchman, that as British Caledonian had placed me in their hotel in town it was bound to be good. Lo and behold, El Meson Royal was a cross between a Greek taverna and a Spanish pension. It was ramshackle, as is the rest of the town, but with a great bar downstairs. I walked into my room with great trepidation to find the towels dirty, the bath covered in pubes, the sheets marked with blood and the air conditioner hanging out of the wall. The lack of loo paper and exposed light wires were minor irritations. I went down to see the manager, a rather obese, gold-clad Lebanese who could hardly raise his hands from his desk due to the weight of gold on his fingers. I showed him my card, BTA Africa desk, and his eyes lit up: Tourism! People suddenly appeared from everywhere, the room was cleaned and polished and much grovelling all round.

I went to the British Caledonian office just before closing and in the fourth cut-out of electricity of the day. I was one of the few white men to have passed through and was royally received. How about a beer... and a second, and a twelfth. The airport manager was just getting over his third dose of malaria in four months and his wife had gone home with cerebral malaria. It was a good evening, the best memories I have of it were spent airing my vocals to bemused locals with a Maori haka. I crawled into bed and crashed only to be awoken by violent shaking. I thought malaria, but no sweats - I turned the tap on and the water was burnt orange. Still shaking I looked out the window to see that the emergency generator had come on and it was attached to my bedroom wall so I sat there and shook until 7.30 that morning. I felt like death warmed up only to be told that I needed an exit visa which took 24 hours and required incentives to be paid to get the photo and the forms. A marvellous day was spent in the heat of Africa trying to battle my way through bemused bureaucracy.

My return trip to the airport cost $40 in bribes and $20 at the airport where I had the good fortune to meet Fr Aniello Salicone, whose desire was a bottle of Lambrusco. He was full of anecdotes – for example, all drivers had to re-take their driving license at great cost, fire extinguishers had to be fitted in the seminary and this required eight lots of paperwork signed by eight lots of people with eight lots of bribes. I undertook to sponsor a seminarian at the father's seminary as I feel the only hope for Africa is for black to help black. He was a warm, delightful man, totally selfless, an inspiration.

Liberia is corrupt. I was told that $28m had gone astray from the previous year's budget and it is in the same league for violence as Nigeria. It's incredibly poor and dirty, yet rich in natural crops. Travellers were stopped at roadblocks 9-5, and at the airport it was a simple matter of 'no money, no flight'. I had to spend three extra days in the country and eventually obtained my exit visa.

This was it!

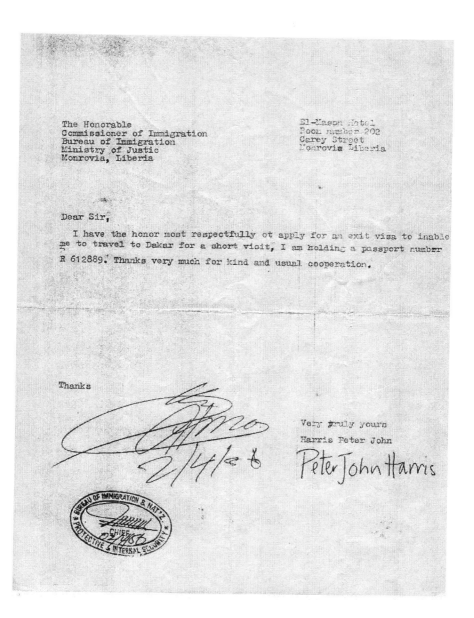

The Honorable
Commissioner of Immigration
Bureau of Immigration
Ministry of Justic
Monrovia, Liberia

El-Mason Hotel
Room number 202
Carey Street
Monrovia Liberia

Dear Sir,

I have the honor most respectfully ot apply for an exit visa to inable me to travel to Dakar for a short visit, I am holding a passport number R 612889. Thanks very much for kind and usual cooperation.

Thanks

Very truly yours
Harris Peter John

Peter John Harris

AND THEN GHANA...

It was one of those exceedingly cold January evenings as I boarded my flight to Accra. The plane was seemingly full of Ghanaians in shabby pinstripes and tatty shirts, loaded down with plastic bags full of junk. I had the misfortune to sit next to two expatriates who were into the sewage business which they talked about *ad nauseam* – embellishing the conversation with a few well-known noises.

Accra hits you as you queue in single lines to pass the immigration official, who spends more time with his nose than with the passports. There is nothing worse than the aroma of stale human pee and hot sweaty bodies at 6am in the morning. Having smelled my way through, I met Steve, the classic grumpy taxi driver, wanting to change money and do a deal. He took me to the hotel, manned by two jaded African women with a solitary expat in the foyer. He said that it was the best hotel in town because it had running water more often than most and some of the sheets were clean. The only problem was the food. There was no restaurant at the hotel and few people ate out – there was a choice of Chinese or Chinese. When my Chinese dinner was delayed, the manager explained: "I am sorry the food was so long but the cook had to go to the toilet with a bad stomach."

Lunch on my birthday consisted of a can of 7-Up, because the burgers at the burger bar were high and my stomach is my master. Most of the food for expats was flown in regularly and this was very much regarded as a lifeline. Most of the Brits I found looked worn out, their previous posts having been Copenhagen and Warsaw. The heat and humidity (98 degrees) were both overpowering and I can understand why 1,000,000 Ghanaians live in Britain.

The British Caledonian manager said he was without a phone for eight months and his home phone had only worked for three weeks in a year. The phones at the British Council had not worked properly for two years and the Japanese company installing a new phone system said they were hindered by the fact that every time they put in new wiring, the locals stole it to use for bangles and jewellery!

THE ZAMBESI EXPERIENCE

I was in Harare for a week promoting British Tourism and meeting the good, the bad and the ugly. I had not been back since my time in the country 20 years earlier on VSO – and now it was Zimbabwe. I stayed at Miekles hotel, a well-known watering hole in the centre of town, and exchanged a seven-day London travel card with the manager in return for an upgrade to a suite. It transpired that nobody could leave the country with more than £300 either on holiday or for good. I vividly remember sitting in the golf club and talking to a very refined colonial lady whose family had farmed tobacco for generations but felt imprisoned in the country because of the financial restrictions.

It has always staggered me that no other black leader in Africa has spoken out against the iniquitous regime and atrocities committed by Mugabe. There would be a massive hue and cry if it happened elsewhere in the world. The Brits made the fatal mistake when carving up Africa of placing the Shona and Matabele under the flag of Rhodesia as they'd been at one another's throats for years.

The UTC (United Touring Company) organization were always highly regarded in Rhodesia for their game tours. The company had been decimated by the change of government but still survived and I really wanted to visit Victoria Falls, so I boarded the bus for a weekend of nostalgia at the Victoria Falls Hotel - a journey back into the past. I spent the first day playing tourist, watching the animals feed, seeing the falls and going to the crocodile farm. I happened to notice in the hotel a day of white-water rafting run by professional expats. I thought, why not? A hell of a way to see the Zambesi. We assembled at 8am, a motley selection of ex-macho men, dubious Qantas stewards, and a selection of women looking for the big thrill! We walked down the canyon along a treacherous path to be told at the end that we were going to ride 16 rapids over 22km. Steve, our guide, placed four of us in the bow and four in the stern and told us that we had no protective helmets or paddles as the rapids were too high and he'd steer into them.

After the first rapid I had that dreadful thought that he didn't really know what he was doing. On closer questioning it transpired that they had only been running trips for three months. On the second rapid we flipped, the bow dropped and we all flew out. I carried on downstream for ten minutes before I managed to clamber out of the river and back into the inflatable. One of the company was 63, 17-stone and wearing a pork pie hat. He got stuck under the raft and came up a deathly grey.

Three rapids later I was thrown out again in a frightening black hole, but we persevered. It was knackering, exhilarating and frightening, all rolled into one. It is not an activity to do with amateurs. At the end of 17 rapids and a number of crocodile sightings it transpired that two people rafting had been lost to the crocodiles on the Zambesi in the previous three months. It was not for the faint-hearted and fortunately there was no newspaper headline: "BTA representative eaten by croc!"

I walked up the steep gully alone to catch the Land Rover back to the airport, thinking what next? *Carpe diem.*

NIGERIA IN THE EARLY '80s

The Foreign Office now advises people not to visit Nigeria unless it is absolutely necessary and I would concur with this view. My arrival in Lagos was hindered by the 'dash' paid in order to get into the country. Each set of officials expected some form of *ex gratia* payment. If you do not pay, your papers are not processed.

I had to cross from the international airport to the domestic airport in order to get a flight to Kano. I was unable to begin with a stay in Lagos as I had planned because the Eko Hotel would not confirm my booking. As soon as we left the airport the driver decided on a somewhat circuitous route through the nearby shanty town. Unfortunately most of the tracks were part-flooded - thus our progress was slow and laborious. Midway through the labyrinth of shacks he stopped the cab and asked me for money. This produced no result so he threatened me physically; still no effect, so he pulled out a gun. Not wishing to be a dead hero, I gave him what cash I had (170 Naira, 20,400 CFA) and he grabbed a bag with my personal belongings in it. Fortunately my ticket, passport and travellers cheques were safe. I got out of the taxi and hurriedly waited until I was able to flag somebody down and make my way to the domestic airport.

Taking a domestic flight in Nigeria is an experience in itself. Most of the flights are heavily over-booked out of Lagos, especially at weekends. On my flight alone there were at least 30-40 people with tickets who were unable to get a seat. It is not possible to reconfirm an internal Nigerian Airways flight. This leads to chaotic situations and varying 'incentives' offered to members of the ground staff. Attendance at the airport at least two hours before departure is obligatory.

In Kano, the hotel had a problem with rats, my room had not been cleaned this century, it had one light which worked, a broken bath, toilet, bed and air conditioner and it took 26 hours to get a roll of toilet paper. The telephone was disconnected and there was no proper lock on the door. On arrival we had a power failure which lasted for several hours and I spent most of this time keeping a 'security person' out of my room. On the second night my room flooded, but fortunately I woke before drowning.

On my return to Lagos I was surprised to see dead bodies on the road in varying states. However, the hotel in Lagos was clean and well run, though one guest had had his door broken down and his personal belongings taken. At 7am I was woken by Frank Harding of Radio Nigeria to be interviewed on the tourist potential of the country. My interview must rate as an African radio classic... I described it as a wonderful country for masochists. Anybody visiting Nigeria in the future would be advised to have a good sense of humour and a supply of Valium. Do not take taxis, especially at night, and never help anybody in trouble. Life has little value in Nigeria.

MORE HAZARDS OF TRAVEL

I had arrived in Nigeria just as diplomatic relations had been restored after the Dikko affair when Britain broke off diplomatic relations and replaced the ambassador with an acting high commissioner. It transpires that when he arrived in Lagos his car was car-rammed on the journey from the airport, a common occurrence in a country where people put steel bars on the insides of windows and live behind steel tensile doors. His driver was forced to strip, then the high commissioner and his wife were also forced to strip by the side of the road, hand over all their belongings and were left there in their birthday suits. They eventually made their way to the high commission and must have had an interesting reception upon arrival.

A similar thing happened to a friend of mine in Sao Paulo many years later. He was car-rammed at traffic lights and the thieves shot him in the leg. He was lucky to live as they hit a main artery, thus he was kept in hospital for quite a long time. When he returned to work after six months his offices had been cleared out and all of the rooms were totally bare. He lost 26 computers and all his files.

I have only been mugged twice, on both occasions in Madrid. I arrived late on a Sunday evening and was reading the newspaper headlines at the kiosk on Plaza De Espana when somebody tipped their change in front of me, I helped pick it up only to have him clear out my front pockets and his accomplice, who appeared from nowhere, took the money from my rear pockets. The following year the same thing happened in the subway but I didn't fall for it this time.

Some years later I visited one of my students in Italy. His father was a hotel owner, and they kindly accommodated us south of Napoli. Liz, my long suffering partner, and I decided to visit Pompeii one afternoon and as we drove down a country lane, a Vespa scooter came across the road from my right in front of the car. I did an emergency stop, thinking I was going to hit him; with that his chum came from the pavement and smashed the rear window, grabbing Liz's bag with her money and passport. Then the scooter driver pulled around to the side of the car, his accomplice jumped on and they were off. We sat there in a state of shock and decided to head for the police station in Napoli, where it became clear this was obviously a common occurrence.

It was 3pm on a Friday afternoon and we were planning to drive to Verona to see the opera, prior to flying back to the UK on the Monday so Liz needed travel documents. We headed to the British Consulate and got there just before closing at four. They were very helpful and said that we needed to get a photograph for the passport but they would stay open. The only photo machine we could find was broken and it took forever to get a photograph. Finally we succeeded and returned to Pompeii at 6.30pm and the gates were closed, apart from the west gate which was open to allow people to leave. We entered unchallenged and spent two hours wandering through Pompeii enjoying a memorable sunset. Then we exchanged the hire car which they nonchalantly accepted and made no charge for damage. *Aida* here we come!

Recently, I was in Malaysia when a colleague was mugged in broad daylight in the city centre. One motorbike came up in front of her and two behind, she was knocked over and her bag taken. On reporting the loss of her credit cards and passport to the British High Commission she was told she would have to pay £148 for an emergency passport and they couldn't seem to understand that she had no money...'tis a funny old life.

BHUTAN'S ONE HORSE TOWN

Thimpo, here we come! When you arrive in Saudi Arabia, as the saying goes, you turn your watches back 500 years. The same could be said of Bhutan.

Twelve of us had raised £39,000 to build a deaf/blind centre for children; the only drawback was that we had to trek across Bhutan to do it. I knew of it as 'the hidden kingdom' and it was next to the Himalayas, and that was about all; they limit the number of visitors per year and you had to spend a minimum of $200 per day whilst in the country.

We flew from Kathmandu to Paro/Thimpo airport and stayed in a slightly surreal hotel on the outskirts of town. Paro can be best described as a film set from a Wild West film. It's a one horse town. People are incredibly friendly and are all dressed in national dress. There are only 700 cars in the country and television was allowed only recently to celebrate the King's accession. Buddhism pervades every aspect of life. The fields are still tilled by oxen with wooden ploughs and there are prayer shrines throughout the country.

Life in the Fens had not prepared me for this; at the age of 50 I wasn't in prime condition. We were going to trek to 5,500 metres (17,500ft) and altitude sickness was a constant challenge with one or two of my group suffering badly before we got to any great height. I discovered that oxygen is limited (54%) which means one had to walk slowly and take a step at a time. I had been given a separate tent as I snore badly and felt that it would be insensitive to try and share as the other occupant would get little to no sleep. It was painful at times getting to the top and this was certainly exacerbated by the lack of oxygen, staying there and coming back down, a challenge second to none.

On our last day climbing we came across the highest school in that part of the Himalayas. As I live near Cambridge and involved in education I was chosen to visit the school the following day as the group's representative. All of the children lined the veranda of the school wearing the national dress, the *llongi*, and sang *Old McDonald had a Farm* in English. I was shown around by a very excited headmaster in the cleanest T-shirt I could muster and my tidiest pair of shorts. The school had very little in it, a few books, broken chairs, failing light bulbs but a wonderful atmosphere. I asked him what the school needed and he came out with a list as

65

long as your arm... winter clothes, books, manual copier, ink rolls, pens, paper. The list went on and on.

When I returned to Ely, where I founded King's International Study Centre, the school community was incredibly generous, especially King's Junior School. My partner, Liz, was very helpful in organising a press release and in allowing me to store boxes in her office. The latter soon became full and I hadn't thought through how I was going to get it all to Bhutan. I phoned a charming chap at DHL, but on telling him there were no roads, only mule tracks, he burst into hysterics and obviously thought that I was a nutter. He did phone me back with a price of £8,500. Liz suggested an interview on BBC Radio Cambridgeshire to raise funds. This was duly sorted but on the agreed date I was overseas so Liz kindly did the interview and took a call from a woman who said her late husband had always supported good causes. She had been moved by what Liz had said and promised to help. A cheque arrived the next day for £8,500. Where the spirit moves...

And the following letter is typical and rewarding.

GONYETSAWA PRIMARY SCHOOL
PARO DZONGKHAG?
BHUTAN.   5/10/2001.

Mr. Peter J Harris,
King's International
Study Centre,
U.K

Dearest Mr. Harris,

        Iam very, very happy to hear from you
that again you are sending some books for my school.
It is good news for my children and they started
shouting and jumping in the air with over joy of
your news.I once more thank you for your kind assist
for my school.

        Sir, my school realy face a problem with
printing machine. A school is a place where it needs
to do lots of printing works of daily activities for
the children. The school and the children would be
very much grateful if, sir could send one printing
machine (Duplicating machine) i.e mannual one. The
Printing machine will be useful for printing question
papers and doing other school works.

        Your supplied tapes and books are highly
appreciated by the school and children and your
further assist will be highly regarded.

Heartiest Regards.

RinZin Wangdi,
Headmaster
G.P.S.
Paro,
BHUTAN.

BEWILDERING JAPAN

Back in the early '70s I was offered an interview by a language school in Shibuya, Tokyo to become its director. I arranged accommodation with Nick, a New Zealander chum who kindly met me at the airport and lived near Shinjuku station. I never realised that any railway station could have 17 exits and all of the names were in Kanji. Each time I got a train I had to count the number of stations and hope that I got off at the right stop. Companies had to send advance information by faxes as there is no semblance of street numbers. They had to tell you which subway exit to take and the large named buildings near their offices.

Nick had agreed to let me sleep on a tatami mat in his kitchen which was most welcome as I was living on the smell of an oily rag in those days, before I recouped my expenses. One evening he took me to the local bathhouse to get cleaned up and this meant going through a myriad of small local side streets. We stripped and caused great consternation and sideways glances as foreigners are genuinely considered to be well endowed. Initially I found the ritual of which bits to wash first daunting but soon relaxed as he left me to go to the laundrette to pick up our washing. Once I got out of the bath house I got incredibly confused and lost. I knew how to get to his small apartment if I could get back to the railway station and catch the appropriate bus. But nobody could understand me. The policeman in his box closed his shutter and people viewed me as a misplaced loony. By luck and coincidence I found the railway station but there were no buses running as it was too late. Fortunately I had the after-hours number for the New Zealand Embassy. Nick had fortunately registered with them and the very helpful lady ordered a taxi to pick me up and take me home. This cleaned me out of yen for the remainder of the trip - but at least I was clean.

I did not get the job and my next trip to Japan was for King's School and at the beginning of February I was in Tokyo again. I had flown with KLM on the southern route and being inexperienced, I didn't realise what that would mean. It meant London - Amsterdam - Vienna - Athens - Dubai - Karachi - Rangoon - Bangkok - Manila and finally Tokyo; and having sat through three complete crew changes no wonder I was feeling so dislocated.

The first trip to Japan is best described as mostly bewildering. The second, much the same. By the fourth visit I thought I was beginning to understand. By the sixth I really understood - understood that I would never understand and that made it all much easier.

The more trips I made and the more agents and students that visited the UK, the more people there were to see in Japan and it was good to find oneself being invited to meet them there. On one trip I judged that it was worth a visit to the southern island of Kyushu - we had by then developed an agent with vague religious connections and he was keen that I should go and meet some school and university principals. He advised that he would make all arrangements for accommodation and so on; all I had to do was tell him my flight number.

I arrived in the aftermath of a tornado - it was hard to tell at a glance if the place was being knocked down, or still under constructions. My man met me and outlined the programme, but first stop was the hotel. Hotel is actually the wrong word. He had kindly arranged for me to stay at the temple with the novice priests – well, it made a change. No bed to be seen, but tatami mats were produced and made up. No bathroom - the bathroom was communal - very! There was a long open wall of showers, a large communal bath and several individual hot tubs, but not a dividing wall in sight. Interesting.

Our agent had arranged two appointments that afternoon and these were at secondary schools and followed a predictable and uninteresting pattern. These done, I was told that the father of one of my previous students had invited us to dinner that night and I should be ready at 7pm when a car would collect me. We returned to the temple. Kyushu at that time of the year was very humid and it was clear, even to me, that I needed urgently to shower and change. My agent reminded me of where the bathroom was and disappeared. A search of my very small room didn't take long and soon revealed the towel I would require. What now? Did I undress in my room and wander about in a towel, or did I undress in the bathroom?

I waited and watched the passageway to the bathroom and soon enough observed bathers going in and coming out, dressed only in towels. I stripped off, gathered my toilet bag and, trying to look confident and familiar, I sauntered to the bathroom. At this time of the day it was now full of steam and Japanese men, surprisingly all more or less naked. I'm not normally embarrassed by nakedness, but this was a first - would these novice priests be uncomfortable with my presence, indeed did they even know I was staying? I was completely ignored, I like to think it was the Japanese way of making me feel comfortable - it didn't particularly.

Circumstances dictated that I had to shower, so with as much aplomb as I could find, I disrobed and strolled stark naked to the showers, feeling very conspicuous, as I realised that I stood head and shoulders over almost all of the novices. The shower was intense, very hot and without controls and so invigorating that I almost forgot that I was showering in the company of 40 would-be-priests. I stepped away when finished and went to pick up my towel, but as I did so, one of the older novices bravely gripped my arm and drew me towards the large communal tub. I indicated that I would rather not and so he pulled me towards the individual hot tubs, where one was vacant. By now I did not want to reject his hospitable gesture, so got in. It was unbelievably hot. No sooner was

70

I in than my new friend dragged-up a heavy wooden lid and placed it over the tub, leaving only my head clear.

It was a very soporific and relaxing experience and I had to be woken by my agent who had become concerned about my absence. I got out with difficulty - my limbs felt unbelievably heavy - they were probably waterlogged. I towelled myself dry and wondered about shaving, but there were no basins or mirrors and I thought of course the majority of Japanese appear not to shave and those that do use electric razors, so I pragmatically decided not to shave and returned to my room to dress.

Both the car and I were on time, but whilst I had been getting very wet inside, so it had outside. I was confronted by rain like stair rods, driving into the ground and making a huge noise and the short dash to the car rendered me almost as wet as I had been in the bathroom. A slow drive through the city in almost zero visibility brought us eventually to the restaurant, although had my agent not told me I wouldn't have known - all that could be seen in the unlit street was what appeared to be a warehouse with one small door, illuminated by a low wattage bulb. The rain was still torrential, so I made a dash for the door and in my haste almost tripped as I rushed to open it. My momentum carried me right into the restaurant, across a small wooden bridge over a stream that ran through it, and I only just avoided plunging into a pool in the middle. My dramatic entrance caused a complete silence to fall over the whole place, but as I got my balance, turned around and released a huge sigh, all the diners burst out laughing and started clapping - don't know which was the more embarrassing. My agent followed more sedately and our hosts then greeted us, trying hard to hide their obvious amusement.

Looking around, it became clear that this was a very exclusive fish restaurant, opulent in the restrained style of the

Japanese and full of extremely well dressed clients. The pool into which I had almost plunged was where the fresh fish were kept and over part of it was the kitchen area. I shuddered to think what the management would have felt if a foreigner had plunged into their food stock. Would their clients still eat the fish?

Pleasantries were exchanged, drinks ordered and delivered whilst we stood in the lobby by the pool. Eventually I was asked what I would like to eat and I politely responded that I was yet to see a menu. Glances were exchanged and my former student came to the rescue telling me that I was to choose my fish from those swimming in the pool. Western squeamishness came over me; I had to pick a fish that would then be killed specifically for me to eat and I felt guilty. I was a coward. I knew that protocol demanded that I choose, but I really didn't want to. Should I close my eyes and point? No, I decided to explain my ignorance of Japanese fish and suggested they choose one that I might enjoy. It was a good decision as they seemed pleased to assume the responsibility and after much discussion, that excluded me, the decision was made and we were escorted away to a private dining room.

My heart dropped - it was a traditional Japanese room - no chairs and for a fairly long-legged foreigner, potential agony. We sat and hot sake was brought and soon the rice spirit helped me forget about the pins and needles that were developing in most of the lower half of my body. Soon, a beautifully dressed waitress appeared bearing a tray of assorted raw fish, boiled quails eggs and miso soup. Eaten and cleared I forgot about my fish to come and more sake reinforced that condition. More food came and went and my lower body became increasingly numb.

Our charming waitress again appeared above us with a wickerwork tray, approached and placed it in front of me - on it lay a whole fish, apparently dead and ready to cook. I assumed it was for me to confirm that this was my fish and that it would be removed before cooking. Wrong, the waitress withdrew and as I looked at the fish, it moved! And then again and as it did so I could see that the chef had thoughtfully cut it into bite sized portions, but not bothered to kill the fish first (I later discovered that this was to prove it was really fresh - a hangover from pre-refrigeration days). I was horrified. I knew there was no way I could possibly bring myself to eat the flesh of the fish, straight from the fish as it were, but equally I knew that it would be very impolite to refuse. They were all looking at me, smiling benignly, anticipating my pleasure, I like to think.

I looked around and suddenly a thought came to me. I turned to my former student and said: "It looks to be a wonderful fish, but I fear my skills with chops sticks will not allow me to do justice to it. Would it be possible to ask the chef to remove the flesh from the bone so that I can eat it more easily?" My young friend replied: "Of course, how thoughtless of us to present you with such a problem, we forget that westerners do not have the same skills as us with chop sticks."

The fish was removed, my face was saved, but I confess I still found it difficult to eat the fish when it returned in pieces, but despite that, it really tasted good. It was still raining when we left the restaurant and the next day when I flew out of Kyushu - I remember the rain, I remember the bath, but what I really remember is that fish.

LOST IN TOKYO

"Do not expect Tokyo taxi drivers to know where they are going as many of them live outside the city."

I read and reread this puzzling entry under the letter T for taxis in my guide book as the airport bus nosed in through the ever-thickening traffic. What, I found myself repeatedly wondering, was the point of a taxi driver who didn't know where to go? Surely a state of affairs as unlikely as a tailor allergic to cloth or a secretary unable to type. I reached into my briefcase and double checked the address to the agency apprehensively. A doddle, they had said. Just pop across to Tokyo, jump in a cab and go and visit old Tadashi. No worries. Got it? I got it. Or at least I had thought I had.

A few days in Japan are not to be sniffed at when you are a young marketing executive and when all I had to do was deliver a load of brochures to our main agent and then head off to Ginza, the Meiji Shrine and the Royal Palace. I had spent the intervening week memorising the main attractions as listed in the only guide book to Japan to be found in our local library. My apprehension diminished as the bus stopped and I headed into the splendid opulence of my very expensive hotel looking forward to a shower and a good sleep.

Next morning, I was wide awake at four o'clock. An hour of fruitless tossing and turning later, I was even wider awake, so in spite of the pitch darkness outside I decided to get up and hit the sights. On reflection, as I shaved with the free razor and shaving cream thoughtfully provided by the management who wished me a comfortable and pleasant stay in a variety of languages, it seemed like a better idea to take advantage of the quieter traffic conditions in the pre-rush hour lull and deliver my package.

In spite of the early hour there was a line of taxis parked outside. I stepped up to the one at the head of the queue and made my first mistake. As I reached for the back door handle the door swung quite unexpectedly open and caught my shins. With a cry of pain I stumbled onto the back seat of the cab and slammed the door behind me, my other hand desperately rubbing my legs. A cry of anguish little different to my own alerted me to the fact that the driver was not happy. In fact, from the gesticulations of his immaculate white gloved hands, I realised that he was really most unhappy. As the rear door mysteriously and noiselessly swung open by itself and then swung shut again with a decorous click I realised my mistake and the reason for the driver's ire.

"I'm sorry," I said. He grunted, turned back to the road and eased the big vehicle away from the kerb, slowly, obviously waiting to hear where we were going. "Do you speak English?"

An expressive and dismissive wave of a glove indicated that he didn't. I reached for the bulky brown envelope and handed it over to him. He stopped the car and turned on the interior light, scrutinising the address cautiously, as if the package might explode. Any hopes I might have still entertained that he would know where I was headed were dashed as I saw his white-clothed index finger trace the words slowly and deliberately along the lines but unfortunately from right to left. I took the envelope back and resorted to trying to read it aloud to him.

"Shibuya." I hoped I'd got it right.

"Uh". Clearly, I hadn't.

"Shee-boo-yaa." I tried it phonetically.

"Uh?"

Not only did he not get it but I could distinctly feel his interest waning.

"Shibuya. Shibuya. Shibuya." I tried it again with a few variations and then, miraculously, I hit the jackpot. He half turned towards me.

"Shibuya." He seemed to pronounce it exactly the same as I thought I had done. Never mind though, he had it now. "Yes, yes, Shibuya," I agreed enthusiastically, only to be rewarded by his voice sounding puzzled once more.

"Ess, ess, Shibuya." He was hesitant. I was frustrated.

"No, no. Not yes. Just Shibuya. Shibuya."

"Jus' Shibuya?" He wasn't following. I breathed deeply and counted to ten.

"Shibuya." I waited anxiously for his response. Mercifully, when it came, it was delivered in a tone of some decision.

"Shibuya."

I nodded wildly but remembered to keep silent. To my intense delight he pulled the column gear change decisively downwards and we were off into the night.

As I rubbed the fast-developing bruise on the front of my leg I checked the address again. This seemed to consist of a series of digits, loosely linked together by hyphens and was not encouraging. A superficial scan of the Tokyo map thoughtfully provided for me by the hotel, who once more took pleasure wishing me a comfortable and pleasant stay in a variety of languages, did little to reassure me as I discovered that Shibuya was seemingly an area about the same size as Manchester. I settled back and watched the lights of the city slip past, remembering that Tokyo taxi drivers should not be expected to know where they were going. If this guy didn't then I wasn't really sure what I should do.

Dawn was breaking as he finally slowed down and stopped. The door swung open and the gloved hand waved in the general direction of 'out'. I could take a hint so I stepped out onto the kerb. I handed through the window a sum of money equivalent to the fare on the meter plus a modest tip and was surprised when the tip was returned to me. For the first time I caught his eye and he smiled, suddenly and disarmingly.

"Shibuya," he said, with another smile, and he swept off into the thickening traffic.

"Shibuya," I echoed with a childish feeling of abandon.

My confidence was not improved as I looked around the confusion of high rise blocks, advertising billboards, neon lights and busy people. Suddenly here I was, stripped of the protective cocoon which the taxi had provided, alone and lost in the midst of a sea of people who all knew where they were going. I took another quick look at the address on the envelope and searched the walls around me for a road sign or any indication of where I might be.

I found myself thinking back to a similar situation in which I had found myself some years previously. On one of my very first business trips abroad I had arrived in Libya to find that the person meeting me had been delayed and so I had to wait. Unfortunately, unlike most other airports around the world, Tripoli airport in those days made no concessions whatsoever to those who did not speak Arabic and so, in consequence, I found myself spending a number of uncomfortable hours unable to understand the loudspeaker announcements, the airport signs and indeed, unable to recognise what might be the toilet, let alone whether it was a gents or ladies. This particular inconvenience assumed more and more serious proportions as the hours dragged by and my relief when my driver finally appeared was to no small degree due to his linguistic skills.

Here in Shibuya I was suddenly plunged into a confusing world where way up above me the skyscrapers bristled with comforting, familiar household names of cars, cameras and electrical goods while down here at street level the few signs visible between the ever-thickening crowds were as obscure in their Japanese script as their Arabic counterparts had been in Tripoli. I struggled for a while through the steady stream of commuters, desperately looking for street names or even numbers on shop doors but to no avail. Finally, with dawn by this time fully broken and the temperature already beginning to climb, I had to resort to personal contact. I selected a girl in her early twenties in the hope that she might recently have studied English and stepped in front of her.

"Excuse me. Do you speak English, maybe?"

If she was surprised to be addressed in a foreign language she gave no sign of it. Instead, she smiled shyly and murmured rather nervously: "A little".

My relief must have been obvious. Beaming broadly I reached for the address of Tadashi's agency and held it out to her. She took it and, screwing up her eyes, read each line carefully, mercifully from left to right, mouthing the numbers to herself as she tried to work out where to direct me. I waited patiently until she made up her mind.

"Follow me, please."

Her English was quite comprehensible and I thanked her profusely as we set off down first one street, then another and then yet another. Finally she stopped in front of a huge modern block upon the smart marble wall of which there were at least some of the numbers from my envelope. We were getting close. I tapped the address with my finger and nodded enthusiastically. She smiled back but didn't look quite as confident as I was beginning to feel. She repeated her invitation to follow her and, together, we circled the block, carefully studying the various combinations of numbers which appeared from time to time around the various entrances. Many of them looked very similar but the exact match for my envelope escaped us.

Returning to our point of departure she obviously felt the need to seek help and found it in the shape of an important looking businessman in a dark blue suit. Together they pored over my sheet, the businessman even turning it over and studying the back in case there might be anything we had missed. After a brief hesitation he led us off along the pavement decisively and we slowly completed yet another fruitless tour of the block. This time, as we returned to the now familiar marble entrance, both of my guides were looking worried.

In the face of such touching kindness, albeit ineffectual, I started wondering what I should say to thank them and let them get on with their lives when, heavens be praised, salvation appeared: a postman. They both pounced on him and the increasingly crumpled piece of paper was subjected to intense scrutiny once again. I stood back hopefully while the postman deliberated but my optimism gradually evaporated as he led the little group of us around the block for a second time. Sadly, it looked very much as though Tokyo postmen shared some of the characteristics of their taxi-driving counterparts.

As we trudged glumly back to the polished marble entrance I was feeling increasingly depressed. Depressed and decidedly embarrassed for my so kind and so willing guides who were clearly deeply upset that they couldn't find the elusive address. The glass doors opened and a man in a lightweight suit strode out, under his arm the unmistakable pink shape of the *Financial Times*. Like a drowning man scrabbling for a life raft I rushed forwards and thrust the crumpled sheet of paper at him urgently. Surprised, he stopped and let me hand it to him.

"Please," my words came out with a rush of desperation. "Have you any idea where this might be?"

He bent forward, blinked and held the envelope closer to his eyes. Then, incredulous, he raised his face towards mine. "Know it? I live there. That's me. This is addressed to me."

The businessman, the girl and the postman looked up, desperately hoping for a solution to our impasse. Then recognition dawned on the other man's face as he realised. "Of course, you're from Exeter, aren't you? I'm Tadashi. That's very kind of you. I was just on my way to your hotel to pick this letter up. Thanks a lot. I hope it wasn't any trouble?"

I looked across at the broad smiles spreading across the faces of my new-found friends, dragged one hand across my bleary eyes and with the other gently rubbed my bruised leg. Trouble? No, not at all.

MICE EMBRYOS ON THE MENU

In Japan, Kita-san has been part of my life for at least 30 years. I had first met Mr Kita in Wimborne in the early '70s as he was one of the two key agents for King's School Japan. He brought a number of junior groups to King's and took some of their leaders to the denizens of Amsterdam to experience some of the seedier spots of European nightlife. I went on to meet Kita frequently over the years and developed a very close friendship with him. Both he and his wife Yoshico loved New Zealand and he was my key supplier of students whilst I had schools there.

He taught me a lot about Japanese culture and life. He wore thick glasses, a dark grey suit with a collar and to get him into surfer shorts and a Hawaiian shirt was a sight to behold. He always enjoyed a good whisky and on my last visit to Japan I took a bottle of Black Label. We consumed it at his club and then staggered to his train. He was mugged thereafter, his computer stolen, and suffered serious brain damage. He has clung onto life for the last six years living in a home and nursed by his wife Yoshico. Love conquers all.

He was and is an eccentric gourmet. On one of my first visits to Osaka he explained that his favourite food was bear paws and mice embryos dipped in honey. I never knew what I was eating in the early days and always prayed that my constitution would hold up.

On one visit to Japan with my new wife, Woodsie, I explained that I was very wary of some dishes and from now on if anything arrived which I didn't like the look of, I would retire to make an international phone call. The first two courses went well, then the waiter appeared and took the cover off the next course with great aplomb. There were mini octopi scuttling around so off I went to make an international phone call. When I returned after ten minutes the cover was still over my plate and Woodsie, with a glint in her eye, told me that they looked so delicious that she'd left me her portion as well, so I had no choice but to eat the damn things.

Many years later I saw Kita-san again and his epicurean tastes had mellowed as his latest pleasure was pasta. I felt quite disappointed.

TAIWAN – AND 'WHERE WERE YOU AT 4.35?'

The train from Taipei to Khaosung arrived at 4.26 exactly. Although I had arrived in Taiwan two days previously I was still a bit sleepy and it took me a couple of minutes to come to terms with the fact that the journey had finished and I had reached my destination. I dragged my suitcase down from the rack, climbed down onto the platform and followed the crowd to the exit.

Outside the station there was a veritable sea of yellow Datsun taxis waiting for the few passengers who elected to continue their journey in that way. In the midst of the cars I noticed a lone grey BMW and wondered who would end up in that vehicle. To my surprise - I was young and innocent in those days - when it came to my turn, lo and behold it was the grey BMW which stopped for me. The driver watched indulgently from the comfort of his seat as I heaved my case into the boot and then slumped gratefully into the back of the car, the air conditioning a welcome tonic. The time was now exactly 4.30.

"Where go?"

His English was clearly streets ahead of my Mandarin. I dug in my pocket and produced the name and address of my hotel. He scrutinised the sheet for a moment and then smiled - more of a grimace really - and set off. I settled back and tried to enjoy the spectacle of block after concrete block and skyscraper after skyscraper. My first impression of the city was, in all honesty, pretty dire but any worries I might have had about the beauty of my surroundings were instantly extinguished when I happened to notice, sticking discreetly out of the parcel shelf to one side of the driver's well fed hip, the very business-like wooden handle, studded with rivets, of an equally serious meat cleaver. This was not a child's toy or some implement he was taking home to his wife as a present -

unless he or his wife harboured seriously homicidal intentions - but rather a chillingly functional killing instrument. I have seen enough Bruce Lee movies to have few illusions about the effectiveness of such a vicious weapon, especially upon a poor, tired, jet-lagged, balding, middle-aged Brit. The sight of the weapon did for me in ten seconds what a syrup of figs takes half a day to accomplish. I crossed my legs, murmured a quiet prayer for my salvation and tried to affect a nonchalance I did not feel. Particularly when he turned to look at me a few minutes later.

We were driving across a wide intersection where traffic lights separated us from the mass of cars running in at us from the right when my driver swivelled his body round in his seat so that he could look right at me. He caught my eye and treated me to a manic grin accompanied by a burst of Chinese. My left eye returned his gaze while my right eye remained fixed upon the well-used handle of the chopper just down to his side. I summoned all the *sang-froid* I could - and I have to confess that it was not so much *sang-froid* as *merde chaude* - and returned his smile with as much enthusiasm as I could muster; probably about as much as Custer when one of his aides asked him if he could speak any Apache.

"Yes of course!" I replied, having no idea what he had said.

He grinned once more and turned back to the wheel mercifully in time to avoid a huge gravel lorry which was pumping a veritable smoke screen out of an exhaust pipe the size of a torpedo tube. I cautiously allowed my sphincter muscles a temporary rest and tried to concentrate once more on the seemingly never-ending succession of shops and office blocks. I was reminded of Dave Stubbings when visiting Houston who made the mistake of asking the receptionist in the hotel where the 'old part' of town might be. The reply was a bemused: 'Gee, I don't think we have one of those.' Certainly, for all I could see of Kaoshiung, there was little of the traditional remaining. But any regret I might have felt at the lack of character of the buildings was instantly replaced by blind terror when my chauffeur turned back towards me once more and treated me to another grotesque leer.

This time he waved a huge fist towards the crowds on the pavement and laughed as he once more subjected me to a raucous outburst of Chinese. I smiled back nervously and began to check the position of the door handles in case I had to make a dash for it. He grinned broadly and returned to his job while I tried to get my heart beat back to just rapid rather than downright ballistic. It was no comfort to me to observe that his neck was actually wider than his partially shaved head and the muscles of his neck and shoulders worthy of a prop forward. As an afterthought I tried to remember how much cash I had with me, as at the very least, I was sure that my taxi ride was going to prove prohibitively expensive, although he was welcome to every penny I had.

It was therefore with quite considerable relief that a minute or two later we swept up to the front door of the hotel, its neon sign one of the most welcoming sights I had ever seen, and he switched off the engine. I was out of the car like a rat up a drainpipe and had manhandled the suitcase out of the boot before he has heaved his not inconsiderable bulk out of the driver's seat. To my amazement he charged me very few dollars, certainly less than any of the taxi journeys I had undertaken during the previous days in Taipei. I dug out the cash, over-tipped him shamelessly and breathed a deep and heartfelt sigh of relief as he grinned once more before returning to the wheel and nosing out into the evening traffic.

Collecting myself and feeling the rush of relief throughout my whole body which almost buckled my knees, I picked up my suitcase and made my way in through the glass doors of the hotel and headed for the reception desk. To my surprise the three people there, a man and two girls, were stunned apparently at my appearance and presumably at my arrival with the mad axeman. I walked right up to the counter and had, quite literally, to snap my fingers in the face of one of the girls before she took notice. Clearly pulling herself together she took my passport, talked me through the registration card and issued me with a kettle. It was now 4.45 almost exactly.

It was with some considerable relief that I reached room 817 on the eighth floor and retired to the toilet to consider the events of the previous 20 minutes. I had no doubt that the mad axeman had come within a hair of murdering me and the near catatonic reaction of the reception staff served only to reinforce my feeling of relief.

Consequently I was not really prepared for the very first thing my friend said to me when he telephoned me some hours later as planned. "Did you feel the earthquake, 6.8 on the Richter scale they say and it happened exactly at 4.35 this afternoon? Everybody in Kaoshiung felt it - indeed even the water splashed out of the toilet bowls in our office - and it was terrifying. You must have felt it, surely?"

So that was what my friend was trying to tell me. So that was why the reception staff looked so shell-shocked at my arrival. It wasn't me. It was the earthquake. I began to feel very foolish.

But it really was a meat cleaver. At least, I think it was - but you don't see them every day in a taxi in Exeter.

THE JOURNEY TO MOUNT ATHOS

Sometimes God moves in mysterious ways, his wonders to perform. I had attended an education fair in Prague and flown on Czech Airlines in the early hours of the morning to arrive at Salonika in Northern Greece at 3am in teeming rain with not a taxi to be seen. Fortunately one eventually appeared and I piled into it with two Greeks going downtown. I was tired, to put it mildly, but the taxi driver only charged me 13 euros and smiled, which helped. The Hotel Virgi, considering the hour, was reasonable. I decided to lie in until 8.30, then go to the Friends of Mt Athos office and check travel arrangements to Sofia.

The bus through the Northern Greek countryside was a joy, rolling hills and abundantly green with a number of severe looking locals. I checked into the Hotel Zeus, tidy, clean and cheap and took a wander around town. Pleasant but very quiet, none of the restaurants had any clients. I pitched up at one, had grilled fish, and spent the night in the grips of violent indigestion. The town came alive in the morning, there were Orthodox monks everywhere, buying goods in the supermarket, taking mobile phone calls and drinking coffee. The boat was due to leave at 9.45 but first one has to get a pass from the Pilgrims Office and purchase a boat ticket. I was tentative and excited to be a pilgrim to such a holy place and somewhat overwhelmed as to what to expect. I'd been inspired to visit from reading *On Top of the Holy Mountain* by William Dalrymple. I knew it was going to be yet another memorable experience. On the boat, I realised that virtually nobody spoke English. The only non-Greeks appeared to be a small group of Germans and two Scandinavians who seemed to possess absolutely every modern piece of tramping gear.

On arrival it was raining and two buses were parked at the quay. I realised I was ill-prepared, had no map, and only knew the name of the monastery. I managed to get on one of the buses, just, and headed off up a very steep incline. It rumbled along making various stops until we got to Karysses where everybody piled off the bus and into a variety of minibuses and antiquated Land Rovers. By the time I got to my Land Rover there were two Greeks in the rear of the pickup who refused to make room for me. All the other buses had left and I was getting very wet. The driver came, threw up his arms, got into his cab and drove off.

I was left thinking, we're pilgrims in a holy land, and this is how they treat a fellow traveller. At that moment another bus turned up. The driver said he was going to Lavra so I hopped in the front. At least I was dry and one monastery must be similar to another. His first stop took an interesting descent on the other side of the island to reach Iviron and the Monastery of Mount Athos. I had actually been booked there on the previous night, but had failed to turn up. So I got off anyway, took my bags and followed the others. Once inside one of the monks asked me where I was from in remarkably good English and asked if I was Australian as he liked Australians. I became an instant Australian - he showed me to the guest master who was just turning away two people who hadn't made a phone booking - I prayed hard and waited as I had come on the wrong night - but he made an exception and showed me to a room with five other beds in it.

Just when I was at my most vulnerable, God had answered my prayers and showed me that if we face challenges we can overcome them. He is there, but even on His own land is still sometimes hard to find and testing our endeavours. A glorious heart, compassion - being turned away from the Land Rover in the rain was one of my most disheartening experiences in a 'special' place - yet God smiles upon you. I was totally dumbfounded that Christians could act in this way. Is salvation from without or within?

As I was leaving Iviron I met a Father who spoke good English. He was French and had joined the priesthood after running a French restaurant in North London for four years. It was only 5.30 am and I said that I was free for the day so he offered to show me some of the 17 monasteries that are scattered on the island. He explained that there were no females on the island and even the cats were neutered. We happened to meet another Australian monk on our journey. He asked me if I was Catholic or Anglican? I responded Anglo-Catholic and he said that was good because he couldn't stand Catholics as they had ransacked Constantinople in 1204 after the second crusade. What hope is there?

HELD IN A GREEK JAIL

From Iviron, I caught the ferry back to the mainland with 101 monks *et al*, then caught the train via Salonika to Sofia. Just as the train pulled into the border post between Greece and Bulgaria we were all woken from our slumbers at 2.30am. Passports were collected by a couple of rather unhappy chappies. The immigration official came over to check something with the two Romanians in the next carriage to mine and then re-appeared with two heavies and told me to pack. I was hauled out of the train and told that according to their computer Peter John Harris was wanted in France. I was taken to the border post and strip-searched and all my belongings and brochures were spread over the floor. My homeopathic remedies and washing bag were spread everywhere. I was then told to pack it up and sit on an extremely uncomfortable, cold metal chair. I sat and sat, whilst Greek police chain-smoked and kept the TV on loud. Nobody spoke any English but I was glad to learn that they had faxed details of both my passports to Interpol and were awaiting a reply. It caused some concern that I'd been to Burma, Russia and Colombia, to name but a few countries, and they obviously thought they had an international crook on their hands; you're guilty until proven innocent.

At 9am I phoned Sofia Education, who were expecting me, and arranged cover for the day. I phoned the nearest British consulate which was closed for the day and then spoke to the British Embassy in Athens, only to be told that I'd just have to sit it out as they had a staff training day. The chair grew more uncomfortable and I wondered how they'd get on if, like most Europeans, they banned smoking in government offices. I was waiting for a fax to come, for Interpol to ring, anything. I suddenly realised how lucky I had been in all my third world travels never before to be incarcerated like this. At least there was one small loo next door, but the place stank.

I phoned Liz at home in England who undertook to alert the Foreign Office to my plight. I sat, walked around in circles, shifts of police changed, my passport was checked again and again. Sitting on two metal seats next to me, two Bulgarians with false passports were yelled at and brutalised. Eventually, after 18 hours, I was taken to be fingerprinted and photographed in the local prison, escorted by two policemen in a car with the siren going. It was like something out of a bad American movie.

A friend, Jonathan, phoned at 11pm to ask if I would be joining other education fair delegates at a disco in Sofia. He heard the goings-on behind me as Romanians and Bulgarians were being beaten and asked if I was at a party! Finally, after 23 hours, I was told that I would be released soon and could be on my way at 2.30am. I decided to head back to the UK rather than face a similar fiasco in Bulgaria.

So here is a copy of the detailed letter I sent to the British Embassy in Athens:

Sacrist Gate House
High Street
Ely
Cambridgeshire
CB7 4JU

I would like to thank you for your assistance following my arrest at the Greek/Bulgarian border in the early hours of Thursday morning 29 April 2004.

I am Director of King's International Study Centre which provides language and study skills for international students wishing to access an education at a UK boarding school. In the course of my job I travel worldwide.

I had booked a sleeper compartment, leaving Thessaloniki on Wednesday evening 28 April to travel to Sophia where I was due to set up and run a stand at an education exhibition.

At 2.30am on Thursday morning (29 April) the train stopped at the border. On examining my passport, I was manhandled off the train by two border police who told me that I was 'wanted' by the French police.

I was stunned, half-asleep and in a state of shock. I was strip-searched. All my bags – I had a large suitcase, a smaller suitcase containing prospectuses and other exhibition material. Everything – clothes, papers, personal possessions – was emptied onto the floor of the police station/border crossing post.

The room which served as a combined reception area, waiting room, interview room was only about 12ft square. There were three metal chairs along one wall. I was told to sit on one of them. A succession of people came and went and the police shift changed at 6am and thereafter every eight hours. My mobile phone was 'dead' and I was not allowed to charge it. I was not allowed to use a telephone or offered any food or drink. There was a toilet next door to the room in which I was held but if I asked to use it I was escorted every time. It was filthy and the surrounding area was piled high with used toilet paper.

At 9.30 am I asked for water but had to pay for it. Eventually I was allowed to charge my phone. I rang the British Consulate in Thessaloniki which was closed for the day, then the Embassy in Athens only to be told that it was a police matter and that nothing could be done. At mid-day I phoned a colleague, Liz Sayers, the school's marketing and media relations officer, and asked her to see if she could make contact from the UK.

By this time I was beginning to feel very disorientated. I was exhausted, fearful, thirsty and hungry. I was offered no food. The atmosphere was very unpleasant. The police smoked incessantly and I was not allowed outside to exercise or to get any fresh air.

It was impossible to sleep or even to doze. Interrogations went on continuously in the same room. I was told that up to 3,000-4,000 people pass through then border each day.

The police detained three Bulgarians, one of whom they handcuffed and physically abused on a regular basis. He sat next to me; panic set in as I didn't know if it would be my turn next.

In the evening at 7pm I was taken to Serres to be finger-printed and photographed in the presence of two border police. At 1am the following morning (Friday 30 April), I was told that my name had been listed as 'wanted' by the Shenken Police – in fact the person

90

they were looking for was a Peter John Harris with the same birthdate as me, formerly of Milford Haven. When my fingerprints and photograph were checked it was obvious I was not the Peter John Harris they were looking for and I was told I was being allowed to leave.

Instead of taking the train to Sofia I decided to wait for the Thessaloniki train as I could not face the thought of there being any possibility of being detained yet again by the Bulgarian authorities (although Bulgaria is not a Shenken country). I was advised to resolve the matter with the French Embassy in London before travelling to any other country.
It had been a classic case of mistaken identity.

The conditions I was detained in were appalling:
• No drink or food was offered.
• Toilet conditions were unhygienic.
• Use of the telephone was not allowed.
• No bathroom or washing facilities.
• Strip lights were on all the time (unless interrogations were going on next door in which case the light were turned off).
• The room was full of cigarette smoke.
• The metal seats were very uncomfortable and there was nowhere to rest.
• There was no area for exercise.
• There was a constant cacophony of sound – shouting and threats.
• The overall atmosphere was aggressive and abusive; 23 hours of sheer hell.

I would have thought that within the EU minimum standards would be observed for anyone being detained; these were conditions of a totalitarian Third World country where fear prevails.

Greece is regarded as the cradle of democracy, and a country which is expecting to welcome thousands of visitors to the Olympic Games this summer.

I intend to take legal advice regarding my wrongful arrest and attempt to take the matter further.

I was left emotionally and physically shattered. I missed an important education exhibition and conference in Sofia, resulting in lost revenue and I also incurred considerable expense.

The whole episode was humiliating, degrading and frightening, a 'living hell' for any professional law-abiding citizen.

I will now contact the French Embassy prior to travelling again.

You did what you could in difficult circumstances. As you might imagine every phone call was overheard. Had I been as frank as I would have wished whilst I was talking on the telephone I was fearful that I would have been assaulted and manhandled in the same way as the Bulgarians who suffered worse than I; as you can imagine every phone call was overheard.

Peter J Harris
4 May 2004

Having arrived back in the UK, I attempted to clear my name with the police in my home city of Ely. The police had never had a case of this type. I was sent to the Foreign Office and had to get various forms in order to clear my name. I was told that I needed to approach the court in France that had issued the initial warrant and ask for it to be annulled. Thus I would need an English speaking French lawyer based in Paris to approach the court in the Paris suburbs to annul the warrant. The cost was going to be 700 euros and because it was a police matter my insurance didn't cover it.

That was it. There was really no point in getting involved in the French legal system and nothing else happened, apart from some coverage of my ordeal in my local newspaper.

EL

Man's 23-hour jail ordeal in Greece

BY Jo Stagg

Email: editorial@elyweeklynews.co.uk

A MAN who was wrongly arrested by Greek border police will go to France to clear his name.

Peter Harris, director of the King's International Study Centre in Ely, has been told by the British Embassy in France that he must appear in a French court.

Mr Harris, 56, was hauled off a train at the Greek-Bulgarian border while travelling to an education exhibition on April 29. He was told he was wanted by French police and held for 23 hours in conditions he described as a "living hell".

Father-of-three Mr Harris was offered no food or drink and witnessed the physical abuse of another detainee. Sanitary arrangements were also substandard.

After seven hours, he was able to buy water and finally allowed to recharge the battery of his mobile phone. He rang the British Consulate in Thessaloniki, but found it had closed, and the British Embassy in Athens, who told him it was a police matter. At midday he rang Liz Sayers, the marketing officer for the King's School, who contacted the Foreign Office.

"By this time I was beginning to feel very disorientated. I was exhausted, fearful, thirsty and hungry. The atmosphere was very unpleasant," said Mr Harris.

Officials realised they had arrested the wrong Peter John Harris when fingerprints and photographs were taken. The two men share a birthday, but the wanted Mr Harris is formerly from Milford Haven.

Mr Harris, who travels extensively with his job and has already made 15-20 foreign trips this year, said: "It has transpired that I have to find an English speaking French lawyer and go before the magistrate that issued the warrant to clear my name."

His passport details and papers were sent to France last week and he is waiting to hear from a lawyer.

The Greek Embassy in London has declined to comment.

■ LIVING HELL . . . Peter Harris, who is going to France to clear his name.

Also, I was told that I would need to keep my report file on me at all times as well as the 24-hour number for an Inspector Duncliffe, their contact at the Metropolitan Police, in case I was arrested again.

Sure enough, a few months later I was detained on the Israel-Egypt boarder for three hours and given a grilling whilst my children were let through; and some years later I took the train from Istanbul to Larissa and my passport was held for an incredibly long time, turning me into a jabbering idiot. I still twitch slightly whenever I am at immigration and am quite paranoid when crossing borders on a train, though 'tis a small price to pay for the joys of travel.

AQUAVITE - AHEAD OF ITS TIME

I have always been interested in slightly mad projects and the Aquavite was one of them.

Hugh Wiltshire, a dear friend of mine who was still professionally driving in his late sixties, had developed a small jet boat in a garage in Poole which could be lifted by two people on to the top of the car and had enough power to pull one adult on a mono-ski. This was in the early '80s and was well ahead of its time in that the Japanese had yet to develop their jet-bikes, etc.

I had met Hugh in Bahrain where he was doing consulting work for Defence Systems Ltd of Albemarle Street. We instantly became friends and I agreed to market his Aquavite project once it had come into production. He had a very talented 'Mr Fixit' working for him and the first trial was quite successful. The jet boat worked and he and I each managed to get up on the mono-ski.

We launched the business at the Southampton Boat Show and then established a sales caravan (which was very much the worse for wear). But Hugh was the true British eccentric. He once lent me a Citroen estate but the tyres needed to be inflated before you drove anywhere. I used it to take things to the rubbish tip where they genuinely thought I had come to scrap the car. Then Hugh needed some office furniture and I said he could have a leather sofa which would not get through the front door and into the lift to the ground floor. So he rigged up a pulley from the seventh floor and lowered it to the ground, much to the angst of my rather precious and affluent neighbours.

At the time of the Aquavite project I was working for the British Tourist Authority in Africa and the Middle East so I was able to take took brochures and information on Aquavite when I travelled. I sold three in Gambia to a hotel chain and a couple more in the Middle East. I made interesting contacts in Japan and Korea, but the jewel in the crown was Singapore. Chris Dakes, a former SBS chum of Hugh's was keen to take a demo model and make it the centrepiece of the Singapore Boat Show. Unfortunately, unbeknown to me, the Aquvite's research and development was still in its infancy. A demo model was despatched to Singapore and with a great fanfare of publicity it was launched – only to survive for 40 minutes before it sank to the bottom.

In subsequent correspondence with Hugh, Chris wrote:

"I must say that the breakdown/failure of the AV at this particular time has caused me considerable embarrassment and possibly loss of sales. I may have mentioned that we were unable to find a sponsor for the Boat Asia Show with Amex TRS and we were planning to run the craft again in the "Sail Past" for National Day (10th August) in their colours. The Sail Past was viewed by some thousands of spectators on land and a million or more on TV: we lost the ability even to take part and have possibly also lost our sponsor now. In addition, we were also due to photograph AV skiing trials in open water for a sports magazine and this has had to be cancelled..."

Shortly afterwards, I arrived in Singapore and having consumed a large quantity of Singapore Slings during happy hour at my hotel, I was taken for dinner at the Singapore Club by Chris and his wife. The atmosphere was tense. It was obvious from the way he talked to his wife that they were having marital problems and I was three sheets to the wind. I ordered, but then was told I had to have the plate of the day and no alcohol as I had fallen on the stairs entering the club. Chris then lambasted me about the failures of the Aquavite and all I could do was take it in good humour, tell him it wasn't the end of the world and that Hugh would make every endeavour to rectify the problems at his factory.

My levity and state incensed him even more. He was at bursting point and it was a great relief to get back to my hotel and stagger into bed.

My friend Hugh is someone with very much a 'can do' attitude and, like me, he has been involved in a number of wonderful ventures – the spirit still moves.

AND THEN... JUST ANOTHER DAY IN THE OFFICE ...

Home again and it is Monday morning, and as usual the phone rings when I am in the bath. This time it is a Polish mother who has lost the phone number of her daughter's host family. "Please phone back after 9.30 English time." Eventually the message is understood.

Time to take my daughter to school. What has she forgotten this time?

Back in time to open the college at 9am and since summer courses start every Monday, the new students are arriving in dribs and drabs. "Good morning, welcome to Harrogate Tutorial College. Please come and sit in the library, the placement test starts at 9.30." They are given their welcome packs to look at while they wait.

The main office is hectic as Kim is wading through a pile of mail, mostly junk but with a few nuggets of interest. The bills and cheques go to Linda, our bursar, who is busy writing cheques to all the host families and some of our suppliers. There have been a few last minute changes due to births, deaths, illnesses, divorces, etc. and Meg brings her up to date. Most of the information on the student notice board has to be changed for the excursions, sports and activities. What a difference Clip Art and laminators make. The horse riders have to be weighed and measured and their details faxed to the riding school.

I switch on my computer and get a coffee while it boots up. Time to check emails, the usual student enquiries, agent messages, announcements of fairs and exhibitions, invitations to spend money on hyperlinks to various web sites and a one-liner from Josh. Peace reigns for an hour, the students are in their classes and the placement test proceeds. This morning the photocopier is behaving. How did teachers ever manage without one?

This summer is relatively quiet. Student numbers are down as the exchange rate continues to work against us. Our agents have explained that the students get more Irish punts for their money, and of course, the Peace Bonus makes the Emerald Isle an attractive destination. Still, it is busy enough.

We are not just an EFL school and several of our overseas students are taking English plus GCSE or A-level courses for university entrance. However, my 10.30 appointment is for a prospective British A-level student. Half way through the interview the noise level rises, the test has finished and the new students are being organised into groups to go round Harrogate. We show them the town and the important services, banks, post office, McDonalds and the rest. The teachers are marking the test and David, our director of studies, is allocating the new students to existing and new classes.

Kim reminds me the minibus is low on diesel and we need to fill it for the shuttle service between the college and the Harrogate Arms. Monday is disco and welcome party night and the venue is just outside the town. A pleasant walk up the hill, but too far for most of our students, who don't like to walk more than a few yards if they can avoid it.

An urgent phone call from an agent - can we accept a group of 30 plus students at two days' notice? This necessitates a lunchtime consultation with David, Janet the assistant director of studies and Meg, our accommodation officer. Yes, we have the staff and classrooms but Meg cannot guarantee accommodation. The local schools break up next week and many host families are unavailable. We make provisional bookings for groups with the families at Easter but with only one student of each nationality per family we cannot manage to place the students. Back to the agent who does not mind if there are several students of the same nationality, even sharing rooms, with the same family? I explain that this is not our policy and not fair to existing students. We are unable to accept the booking and please give us more notice next time.

A minor panic occurs. A coin has stuck in the snack and sweet machine in the common room and the staff coffee machine is not working properly; deprived of sugar and caffeine, the college would not function. While I'm in the staff room, we have a quick conference about an aberrant student, then it's time to go home for a sandwich and back for afternoon classes. The new students are shown their classrooms and meet their teachers. Janet's class come down to the computer suite and no doubt will be on the internet, Cathy's class are going into town to do a survey, but are fortunately too intimidated to question me. I am back on the computer replying to enquiries, reassuring agents and completing a couple of questionnaires.

We are also running an IT course for teachers in local schools and Steve, our IT expert, has just finished cleaning up the computer memories and loading Windows 98. The computers can only access the internet with a smart card and Steve and Janet go round with the cards. The students see the student pages on our web site and want to write their own. It is a great incentive for them to write correctly and accurately for a global audience.

Monday's routine continues, the disco tickets with the one free drink entitlement are being updated and printed on the colour printer. It should be a good disco, the current students are very pleasant and friendly and the DJ has a stock of Europop, which he has built up in response to student requests. The photocopier is churning out maps and information for this week's excursions, a half-day in Bradford for ice-skating, the Museum of Cinema and Television, and a full day in York.

A student wants to change his host family. Meg spends some time trying to establish the cause of the problem and then goes to see the family. She has the patience of a saint and copes admirably with the interminable phone calls. She will also visit two prospective new families to look at their homes and explain the guidelines and their responsibilities. It does not matter how good our courses may be, if the students are not happy with their host family they will not enjoy being at the college.

It's time to make a quick phone call to ARELS (the Association of Recognised English Language Schools) about the workshop in September. The update on the agents attending will be on their website soon and they will give us the access password; then it is email and fax time again to make appointments. My schedule is starting to fill and I hope it won't be as busy as my trip to Berlin with 50 twenty-minute appointments in two days. You only get to see the city from the hotel and taxi windows at these marketing functions.

Time to relax and look through some of the new web sites. Free offers to participate for two months with hyperlinks and the new JKM GoUK magazine has just come online. There's a lot there and Josh has included our press release as well as that of the Language Academy. Two for Harrogate, I can't complain about that.

I finally leave the college at 6.15pm, the phones are not being diverted to me tonight so no calls at 3am from people trying to send faxes on the wrong number. Steve will pick me up on the fast shuttle-run to the disco (gone are the days when I used to drive the minibus for the disco and airport transfers). In the early days of the college we even used to pick up students from Heathrow. These days I drive on the motorways as an absolute last resort.

At the disco it's good to see some of the teachers, who are not on duty. Linda and Kim are there too, and they'll all get an additional free drink. Janet is there with her children. My daughter joins them and they disappear into the grounds.

That was just Monday!

THE TURKISH PARROTS

While I was with the British Tourist Authority (BTA) part of my brief was Turkey as well as the Middle East and Africa. It was a burgeoning market, especially for English language schools and thus in 1985, I organised sales missions to Istanbul and Izmir with a colleague, Chris Watton. They were hard work, great fun and exceedingly well attended. Barry Henwood of MLS had signed a contract with several Turkish mayors which kick-started his business and John Adams found a memorable representative in a local beauty parlour. All did well.

Agent visits were organised on one particular day and I took off for Bodrum with John Adams as the mayor had invited us to see the land which he wished to transform into a golf course... it was the local rubbish dump. John, who was and is, a very good golfer trudged over the debris until lunch time when the mayor invited the chap clearing the drains outside his office to join us, adding a distinctive aroma.

On our penultimate day I organised a trip to the Temple of Ephesus where John Miles and I decided that we should continue the fun and spread the joy of cricket. We would form a cricket team consisting of those who knew how to play, and those who didn't but just loved the game. In order to join the Turkish Parrots (as we named the group) you had to be able to name the Seven Wonders of the World - Ephesus, the Temple of Diana and the Mausoleum of Halikarnassos all came to mind, as did the Temple of Alexandria. We never got the full seven but Worcestershire cricket pavilion somehow crept in.

The British Airways flight back from Izmir was memorable in that we drank the plane dry and the Torbay town crier created a wonderful party atmosphere for one and all, ringing his bell up and down the aisle.

John Miles followed up with this letter to all our friends, which clearly defines the objectives of the Turkish Parrots!

Dear

Following our highly successful (well, it was for the rest of you) sales mission to Turkey in February and the presentation of the 1986 Golden Parrot Award to Norman Harris in Izmir, the Turkish Parrot Club has now been formed.

We are working on the statutes and they are proving particularly tricky (how to fit in gherkins, marmite etc?) but you should receive an official invitation to join within a couple of weeks. Our activities will be mainly gastronomic, alcoholic, sporting and in the spirit of the Turkish mission. For a measly joining fee you will be able to sport a club tie and a club shirt and have access to some extraordinarily revealing photographs of the committee (messrs P. Harris, J. Adams, J. Miles, C. Watton). Any surplus proceeds to charity!

The urgent pupose of this letter is to ask if you would be available to play cricket for the Turkish Parrots XI against the Bournemouth All Stars XI on Sunday May 25th, Meyrick Park, Bournemouth, 2 p.m.

As time is short, please ring me on (0227) 728318 any evening after 12th May and let me know if you are available.

Please try and come! This should be the inaugural meeting of the Turkish Parrots, one you cannot afford to miss!

Yours

John Miles

P.S. We have taken into account the fact that you cannot play cricket to save your life and we still want you. Don't worry, John Adams can't play either!

I was chair of governors at Pamphill School near Kingston Lacey in Dorset at the time. The school overlooked a wonderful tree-lined cricket pitch and thatched changing room, with a pub in walking distance. In that idyllic setting, we played a number of games against teams ranging from Chelsea Arts XI to Corfe Castle Bakers. It was all 20 overs starting at 2pm and finishing by the time the pub opened. I worked with Dave, an Aussie fast bowler from the hinterland of Queensland, who brought along his mate Bruce, an opening bat and they frequently supplied the backbone to the team. It was a mixed array of talent but a thoroughly enjoyable interlude in our lives. Some took it seriously and certain lbw decisions still rankle today.

Over the years, we played more games and were offered a private pitch beside the sea at Studland, so that families with children could romp on the sand. When my children were very young we accepted a fixture against Guttsta Wicked Cricket Club in Sweden. This was a brewery owned by a Swede who had been educated in Britain and developed a love of cricket. When we got to the ferry we realised that Danny Fewtrell, my 'odd job' man, didn't have a passport so we had to smuggle him across under the kit bags, both there and back. It was quite a journey! We got slaughtered as some of their team were antipodeans who had driven 700kms from the Arctic Circle for a game. We were depleted in numbers and my son, Ollie, and daughter Sophie, had to play as well.

One person who played in every match was Danny. He was an incredible sportsman and was naturally gifted with bat and ball. He also endured cancer of the stomach and bladder, meaning frequent hospital visits. He had two young children and every time he went into hospital he lost part of his benefit. He would come and play cricket after a session of chemo. His attitude, toothless grin and his humour were an inspiration to us all and we ended up curtailing our philanthropic activities to help Danny. He was one of the major reasons that I started scribbling in the first place with the aim of donating any proceeds to Danny or to a trust for his children. The Turkish Parrots also had an early Christmas lunch at the RAC at Woodcote Park where everybody donated generously but we all enjoyed the deckchairs, willow and camaraderie over the years.

My 11-year-old daughter, Sophie, decided to get in on the act and, without telling anybody, wrote to The Queen! Here is the reply she received:

PALACE OF HOLYROODHOUSE

6th July, 1999

Dear Sophie,

I am commanded by The Queen to write and thank you for your letter.

Her Majesty was interested to hear that your father is compiling a book of travel stories, but as The Queen receives many letters and requests each day, I am afraid it is not possible for Her Majesty to reply to them personally, or to do as you ask.

The Queen was, however, so sorry to learn of your father's friend, Danny, and hopes that the book will be a great success in raising money for Danny and his family, and for cancer charities.

I am to thank you again for your thought in writing to Her Majesty.

Yours sincerely
Mary Louisa.

Lady-in-Waiting

Miss Sophie Harris

103

FINALLY, MY ENCOUNTER WITH ANOTHER WAY OF LIFE

We are very much creatures of our own making and upbringing. My father had quite liberal views for a man of his ilk. He believed in homeopathy and was a passive naturist, genuinely believing that exposure to the sun was good for us; he even took us to a naturist camp on the Isle of Wight as children. We didn't know where we were going and were met at the front door by the owner, a single-parent, and his 14-year-old son, absolutely starkers! My initial reaction as a 12-year-old was "I am not showing my plonker here!"

I knew nothing really of sexuality. It was the end of the 'children should be seen and not heard' era and, apart from talk about a used condom which blocked the cesspit in Winfrith when I was a 16-year-old, sex was never discussed. A master at school was dismissed for fondling boys in the scrum; my Aunt Ella had left her husband on her honeymoon, methinks because she saw his plonker, to go and live with a female friend and I remember asking my mother why Dirk Bogarde had to leave England with his secretary to live in France and she was exceedingly flummoxed.

As a teenager hitchhiking in France I had been picked up by a chap in Belgium who asked me if I would like to go for a swim and as it was a hot day I agreed, only to strip off and see the 'Eiffel Tower' appearing. I pulled out my travel knife - a small Swiss Army knife I always had handy - just in case. It's the only time in my life I've ever had to do so, and the 'tower' collapsed.

In my wayward years and my early thirties, I was still single and had a very active social and sex life. Suddenly, there was an awkward change in society; gays came out of closets and there seemed to be large numbers of young men dressed like army

104

corporals in civvies with small Hitler-like moustaches, although the mood was somewhat subdued by the onset of Aids. I, like so many, was thoroughly bemused - suddenly there were gay bars, gay travel and meeting Michael Donald opened up that world to me.

During the early 1980s, I was on an educational marketing trip to Bahrain and Dubai. This was when I first met Michael who had worked and lived there for a number of years. He was interested in establishing an English Foreign Language school. On our first meeting I was wearing a safari suit with a signet ring on my little finger and, as I was in my mid-thirties and unmarried at the time, he assumed I was gay. Being of a kind and generous nature he invited me to stay at his flat. On arrival I was somewhat taken aback to find him adorned in a gold, embroidered dish-dash with a slit up the side. He asked me if I was a 'swinger'. By the look of bewilderment on my face he could tell I wasn't. We came to the arrangement that I'd stay but when he was 'entertaining' he would leave a plant pot between the curtains. It rarely moved as it soon became clear that his nights were as busy as his days. He arranged a party on my first Friday night. Everybody came in drag and there was just one girl - just in case I really was straight. I didn't leave her side all night.

However, Michael became a wonderful friend and taught me a lot about a world I'd never known. My eyes were well and truly opened. He lived opposite the police training school and could be found most mornings on the balcony eyeing up the new recruits with binoculars. We had cause to visit the police station once and walked up to the guard on the door whereupon Michael kissed him fully on the lips and we strode through.

I received a number of letters from him over the years and here is just an extract from one which he headed 'Gay Sunday' and in which he recalls the late Terence Higgins who did so much in his short life to create awareness of Aids:

As I sit here typing this epistle there are strange sounds coming from a cage at the other end of the shop... she looks like a parrot, eats like a parrot... but I am convinced she is a reincarnation of my old friend Terry (he died of Aids two years ago) and he swore he would make it back... you may read about him sometimes in the newspapers. He was unfortunately one of the first to die. A Trust has been set up and is often mentioned... the Terry Higgins Trust... I often think of him and remember the days and weeks I spent hitch-hiking through Europe with my sling-backs in my rucksack and Terry sitting on the back of military trucks... with his legs crossed... he did enjoy life and knew he would not have a long one. He often said he would never see 40... well, he died at the age of 36. I shall always remember him as the guy I first met and not the man I saw at the end... I was at the airport waiting for him to come through immigration and when I saw him I thought... My God... she has back-combed and lacquered her hair... I mean, it was so obvious... as he went through the door in front of some very amused Brits he said: "Hey Gladys, do you realise I am using Harmony hair spray." Well, I fell about and I immediately started to swing my hips and dropped my wrist...

The letter goes on... but this extract illustrates his extraordinary personality. I am sure his letters to me were therapeutic, but after a while, all went quiet.

A number of years later, I worked at the British Tourist Authority and out of 11 couples attending a theatre preview night in London I was the only man with a woman. How times had changed! Now same sex couples have civil rights which can only be a good thing; though if I'm honest, I still harbour the view that most women just need a good bloke, which could class me as a male chauvinist pig. I really wonder what women see in one another sexually but, I suppose, love conquers all.

Glyn, a great friend, once arrived at a house in Clapham where I was staying, with grass stained knees, only to reveal that he'd been 'cruising' on Clapham Common... and I thought that he'd been out house hunting!

PART 2:
PEACE, TRANQUILITY, ENLIGHTENMENT

BUCKFAST ABBEY

What brought me here I know not. We had been staying in a challenging bed and breakfast near Dartmouth run by an ex-naval commander and his wife. It was 1984 and Woodsie (my ex-wife) and I had decided to spend Easter weekend in Devon. It rained constantly, and the room at our bed and breakfast room was cold and damp and the chair, according to the good commander, had been attacked by rats! Woodsie managed to burn her socks on the very ancient heater. Our visit was saved by an excellent soup but we departed early rather than face the threat of a 45-minute walk with our host down to the beach via the cliffs (he had recommended a place for a jolly good prawn sandwich at lunchtime).

En route, we stopped at Buckfast.

I am not Catholic and if a label must be used I would call myself an Anglo-Catholic; perhaps it is just easiest to say I believe in God, am tolerant of all faiths and enjoy a certain degree of ritual smells and bells. After attending the Easter service there, I knew that I had to return; whether it was a monastic or iconoclastic pull from a previous life I know not, but return I did and was welcomed with open arms by a number of the community. I have now been coming to Buckfast for 30 years and usually make it back twice a year, usually in spring and late autumn. Why? Its utter simplicity, the silence and the friendships. I live, by choice, in a world which is frenetic and full of movement; here the brakes are on. The beauty of vespers and compline is uplifting to the body, soul and spirit - even to one who just scraped through O-level Latin and with a limited knowledge of the Gregorian chant and plainsong. The community is probably no different from any other of its type and there is tremendous discipline in the lifestyle.

Finding Buckfast was perhaps the first stop on my own journey of enlightenment - it is a bit like a river which started off as a slow stream. I meandered for many years as I drifted there in between my frequent overseas travels, as I covered 109 countries in Africa, Turkey, the Levant and the Middle East - excluding South Africa and Israel - as the British Tourist Authority representative for the region. It made me think of things spiritual, of being, of compassion and gave me an appreciation of the power of silence.

The first time I visited Buckfast there were hot plates at a self-service lunch. I sat awestruck as one monk after another on zimmer frames attempted to pick up hot plates and juggle them and the zimmer! Charlie Chaplin would have been proud.

Buckfast has been the strangest friend over so many years and I have got to know a number of the monks extremely well. I have spent many happy evenings with Father Sebastian after vespers in his cell sharing a medicinal glass of Jameson's before compline. From time to time he would play his latest piece of organ music. The last piece had a South American rhythm... what joy to listen to it. It reminded me of the cinema when I was a child, with those large Wurlitzer organs pounding out their beat.

Sebastian is now 86, in frail health but strong spirit. To celebrate the Golden Jubilee of his ordination, the director of music at Ely Cathedral, Paul Trepte, kindly played some of his organ motets at matins which was a wonderful touch of ecumenicalism.

Perhaps one of the most wonderful man-made creations to sit and look at is the figure of Christ at Buckfast Abbey, created by Father Charles Norris who was the oldest living monk in Britain when he died at 94, though a number of his colleagues there are not far behind him. He used a French technique (*Dalles de Vere*) whereby very thick glass is set in concrete to make up pictures and thus whole walls can be built up like a mosaic of coloured glass.

Father Charles has been a blessing in my life - an incredible talent; the sheer magnificence of his stained glass which is in the chapel is second to none. He worked in a dilapidated hut and produced the most exquisite work. His trusted assistant, Father Paulinus, approaching 94 himself and unable to see much, was still very alert.

I got to know 'Father Poly' very well over the years as I sent him books to improve his English for which he was most appreciative. He's an Egyptian Coptic monk from the southern deserts. I asked him about life as a monk and he saw himself as a spot of oil in a pool of water which I found to be a pleasing analogy. I asked him to speak at Ely Cathedral to the international students at King's. They were astounded that he had chosen a life of hardship in the desert as a monk rather than practising as a doctor. While he was giving his homily, his mobile phone went off, causing great embarrassment. One Japanese student later told me that he was most impressed that God had phoned him while Father Poly was speaking.

Father Charles fell quite badly down stone steps some years ago and suffered mild concussion. He had to have a number of stitches; he moved into the village with a nurse and sadly passed away. Right to the end he still went to his workshop most days in the morning and was very active - quite an inspiration. His days in North Africa and Italy during the Second World War, and on the hospital ship from North Africa to South Africa, are the essence of a good novel.

The funeral for Father Charles was incredibly touching, an incredible man whom it had been a privilege to know and spend time with; he left for his meeting with his maker on a 19th century hand-drawn coffin bearer, surrounded by monks singing Gregorian chants, on a lovely summer day where the blue of the sky matched the beauty of his stained glass windows.

ESCAPISM? COMMERCIALISM?

I often thought of the monastery as escapism which on one level it is but, as I grow older I realise that the happiest and most balanced people I've come across have moved beyond the physical, mental and emotional and sought the spiritual. You don't need to go to church to find the latter. I do and I find it there but I am well aware of many people who are on a spiritual path but have turned away from the church.

Buckfast continues to draw me back like an umbilical pull, year after year; it's like a battery which regularly needs to be topped up and re-charged. The joy of simplicity. Brother Joseph was the guest master in my early days there and he took exceedingly good care of all retreatants. It's a sobering experience to be with people who have given all material things away and yet still continually give of themselves.

I genuinely take the view that the House of God has many doors and it doesn't matter which door you enter as long as you enter one. That is why, although I have great empathy with many of the tenets of Buddhism, I could not become a Buddhist as it is essentially non-deistic. Sai Baba, whom I'll come onto later, is of greater appeal: love all, serve all and act with compassion and love. Be tolerant.

Yes, my spiritual journey started at Buckfast and looking back I see the roots. I was clinging onto the logs at the side of the river and wouldn't let go; once I did I began to experience another unforgettable journey.

Commercialism has been the lifeblood of Buckfast as it needs to survive in a changing world. To some sceptical souls it became known as 'Fastbuck Abbey' and there was a certain degree of consternation in the '90s when the school and village shop were closed as, under the tenets of St Benedict, education is of primary importance. The old village school is now used as a conference centre and through the year it is used for a wide variety of activities. I was always hopeful that one day it would be used, in part, as a healing centre for mind, body and spirit.

Then there is the success of Buckfast Tonic - a red wine-based aperitif which is 15 per cent alcohol, costs just £5.49 and is now widely distributed. Born out of religious devotion, it is believed that the original French monks who settled in Buckfast Abbey in the 1880s brought the recipe with them. It is still used today. It is largely drunk by the young and underprivileged. But research at Polmont offenders' institution in West Lothian revealed that more than 40 per cent of those who had consumed alcohol immediately before committing their crime had been drinking Buckfast Tonic. Scary stuff. But sales of the drink - whose unofficial catchphrase is 'made by monks for drunks'- have soared to £37,000,000 in the past five years, with Scots spending more than £50,000 a day on it. It seems some just can't resist the lure of a bottle of 'Buckie'.

A FRENETIC CONVEYER BELT

Everybody at some stage needs to retreat and lick his or her wounds. We all need help and the appreciation that the answers are within us. I've always been a somewhat wayward spirit, acted impulsively and been driven by great curiosity. As I wrote earlier in

Part 1 of this book, my life has been a wondrous adventure and discovery. The riches of spirit have been paramount and the desire to pull down the brick walls which surround and limit me and most of us.

Mankind is carried along on a frenetic conveyor belt of hype and illusion assuming that all can be achieved by the acquisition of material wealth. I can't and never will submit to such thinking. Peace of mind for many comes through silence, the ability to stop the monkey brain. Give and you shall receive, as the saying goes. If we were as driven by the same desire to know our inner selves as we are to make money what a wonderful world it would be. Since time began we have all needed shepherds to lead us, now we have politicians who, like the former American President George W. Bush couldn't conserve and look after the world's resources, but felt a constant need to plunder them. Why not look for alternative sources of energy? We cannot and should not rape the environment. Man must look into his heart and speak candidly. The truth hurts but it must be said.

Modern man is losing the ability to be grounded and balanced. To many of us, imbalance causes disease and that is the beauty of complementary medicine, like kinesiology, which balances the individual. We should change the way we look, see and live. I would like to see tithing re-introduced whereby ten per cent of what a person earns is given to charitable causes. This is effectively done by the Church of the Latter Day Saints. Many are becoming victims of donor exhaustion, every other letter seems to request some form of cash. Employers could be encouraged to release staff one day per week, or even half a day, to help with the street kids or homeless or some social cause. We should 'walk the talk' as the Americans would say.

So many of my fellow Christians feel as though they are part of some elite group which will be on the first bus to be saved rather than fully appreciating that instead, we should be out in the communities giving ourselves, which is just as important as genuflecting. How many of our clergy spend endless hours in committee meetings rather than being out among the people where they are so desperately needed? Fear pervades our lives. Old people are scared. Police drive round in Panda cars and are never on the beat, our clergy are rarely seen in the community, society is somewhat rudderless, although one is aware that the onus ultimately falls on the individual.

To be at a crossroads in life is a common occurrence and we must endeavour not to lose the power of the spirit within. We know the answers yet find it difficult to accept them. The conflict for many is being driven by the ego rather than by the power of the spirit. A haze frequently clouds our thoughts and the monkey brain is one of our greatest challenges as we become obsessed with doing rather than being.

Consumerism drives many with the pressure of 'must have' constantly feeding the craving, but for what? We crave for simplicity, being grounded and open to the rhythms of the seasons, the sound of the birds and the joy of God's creation. Just as seagulls overhead remind one of the sea, Gregorian chant lifts one to a point between earth and heaven. Why are we here? What are we trying to achieve? Modern man has lost his or her way and life is reduced to a helter skelter or a waterwheel with a donkey going round and round. Disillusionment is a common fact of ageing, look around and see the dumbing down in every aspect of our lives, the tabloid expressions of so-called 'quality' newspapers, youngsters covered in tattoos and body piercings, reality television and obesity. Somehow we've lost our way, we're out of kilter with the rhythm of life. It is a disposable world.

Spending time at Buckfast, you realise that the community there is faced with exactly the same problems as the 'outside' world, though it has been transformed over the last few years and now has a director of music and the Abbey Choir. A number of younger men have joined the community and a vast amount of money has been spent refurbishing the Abbey for its jubilee celebrations in 2018 for which Father Sebastian is writing a major organ opus.

WALSINGHAM – RELIGIOUS TOURISM?

This was an unexpected challenge on life's rich path. I arrived at Walsingham at 5.30pm on a Monday to get my room key and to be given a brief of the daily routine. It was very informal but in keeping with the place.

I walked over to the accommodation area with my wheelie bag in the constant drizzle. A welcome meeting had been taking place in the lounge; suddenly the door opened and 11 electric chairs and wheelchairs emerged with pilgrims in need of the healing powers of the shrine. I walked down the corridor and through another lounge to find my room, to be met by a cadaverous-looking man slumped in a chair who looked and spoke in monosyllables as though he was not long for this world. I wondered what on earth I had walked into.

My room was small but adequate with two adjoining loos for the whole house and there was no mobile phone connection. I went back to reception and was told that if I stood next to the altar in the garden and leapt in the air, I might get one.

I had missed mass/vespers so I went to supper. The restaurant was full, 300-plus people, mainly elderly, sick and obese. I sat on the staff table and mentioned the interesting variety of people and was given an account of the challenging people who came here, especially the lady who couldn't sleep in a bed and had to have a chair in her room.

The focus here is on the Anglo-Catholic Church where some who have been ordained in Oxford are called by their mother's Christian name, so I amused myself by wondering who among them was called Gladys or Myrtle. The priests had come from far afield with their parishioners to participate in the healing aspects of being near Our Lady and having water sprinkled from the Holy Well.

I slept well, rose early and went to 7.30am mass, which was full of schoolboys from a well-known public school with their chaplain and art master, as well as a cross-section of the deeply religious and needy.

Walsingham seems to act as a magnet for the unusual and challenged; the accommodation smells of old ladies. God does have a sense of humour... one appreciates the vitality of religion here as one feels the needs of the sick and the elderly. 'Tis challenging. Sometimes in life you peer over the other side and see how you might end up. I have never seen so many disability scooters, zimmer frames or sticks in one place.

It's very strange being exposed to group religious tourism. People stick to their own parish groups which is understandable, with very little bridge-crossing or inclusiveness of others. I found it fascinating to be with such large numbers and yet be alone. People today are apt today to look inwards rather than part with a few welcoming words. The one exception was at a healing service where the priest asked the congregation to speak to somebody they didn't know – and when it happened the whole place was soon abuzz with conversation.

The early morning mass appeals to the religious groupies who frequently wear black with large crosses and sandals, crossing themselves at every opportunity. There is constant movement in the gardens with various groups visiting and reciting at the 12 Stations of the Cross before they go on to the local religious 'tat' shops which abound. If people would only smile life would seem lighter and more bearable. Sometimes words touch you and the homily on this day was on being authentic rather than perhaps being in the picture we all try to paint. Does being more fervent make us better people? Possibly, but the jury is out.

This is like a large religious supermarket, overcrowded and to me, lacking a real sense of spirituality. I am sure it is there and in the shrine one is aware of the presence of a certain energy. A sign of the modern age was to see a vicar, his wife and parishioner all sitting in the lounge using their mobiles (they found a signal!) and not a word spoken.

MEETING MOTHER MEERA

So many of us live empty, soulless lives because we crave popularity, appreciation, and praise, and have lost contact with sunsets, good books, good movies, enjoyable work and good company. I remember sitting at a dinner party with all the props and trappings of success, thinking that something was terribly lacking in my life and I genuinely could not put my finger on it. Over dinner we talked about a vast range of topics and somebody asked if I had heard of Mother Meera. It transpired that eight out the 12 people there had all been to see her. I was hooked, though I wondered how could an Indian based in Germany, who at the time had written one book, entitled *Answers*, attract to her people from middle class countries?

Mother Meera (an Indian avatar and a source of divine light) is based in Balduinstein, a village in southern Germany, where one is aware of the affluence, with all the trappings of wealth that pervades the place, but the people seem sad and fail to smile. We walked to Diez, a small town on the river. It was a riverside walk of one and a half hours each way, two people among of the countless cyclists and walkers who failed even to acknowledge us, too busy wearing the right gear and looking troubled. It was a joyous day and a sheer delight to see the sun shine and the leaves, burnt orange, glistening on the trees... perhaps we all have too much.

I was drawn to Mother Meera four years ago and have been visiting her twice a year ever since, much to the initial chagrin of my wife who found it difficult to accept the spiritual faith I was following on a number of levels and really blew a valve when she discovered that I had also undertaken a reiki course. At the end of the day we all have our path to follow and must do so, whatever the initial consequences. Love must penetrate all of our actions and forgiveness should be to the fore.

Meeting Mother Meera is described by some as an encounter with a spiritual vacuum cleaner. Every experience with her is very different. One sits in a large hall with 200 other people meditating and then form a queue for a laying on of hands as you kneel before her and she stares into your inner soul. My monkey brain usually works overtime but what is fascinating are the dreams and images some experience after Darshan (silent meditation). On one occasion it was similar to having an electric shock pass through me. The majority of people there are now German though a number of years ago it was an eclectic international mix. It is organised and run with Teutonic efficiency; woe betide if you are late, and now a number of people attend Darshan dressed in white, as if they were attending an ashram. The thing that always strikes me is the lack of joy on people's faces. Here we are, attending 'mother', and one gets the feeling that a majority of people are exceedingly troubled. There are also the regular groupies who must go every weekend, which is somewhat troubling.

I experienced Darshan as a re-charging of the spiritual batteries, a chance to be grounded and look inwards. I sometimes wonder if we spend part of our adult years start looking backwards to our childhood years and the uninhibited powers we possessed as children? So frequently one hears that you can have everything and nothing. . Therefore most of us experience that as we start outwardly on life's rich voyage. Madonna, the pop singer now in her fifties, attracted newspaper attention when she said that she doesn't allow her children to watch television and they can watch films only on Saturday. For a woman who has lived in excess, made some questionable films, and now deprives her children of freedom of choice, this is bizarre, for surely we need to educate our young to be tolerant and selective?

Mother Meera... there is silence and power... and what joy! Mother Meera, even to the cynical, has an aura which is palpable and as she enters the room there is electricity. One sits for up to two hours meditating, clearing what Sai Baba would call 'the monkey brain'; then one kneels before her and there is a laying on of hands. The experience each time is very different... here are some of her words:

> *The heart is a flower that needs to open*
> *This too shall pass*
> *Perhaps we all observe the truth, there is never enough time*
> *as we hurtle headlong, onwards.*
> *We must live in the now like the river, everything returns.*
> *God is everywhere.*
> *Have the moral courage to be who we are.*
> *It's not life that matters but the journey.*

Assert and express your feelings honestly, openly and
lovingly.
Be inspired, write.

And so I wrote:

My Hope
I will be capable of loving,
Regardless of whether I am loved in return.
Of giving, when I have nothing,
Of working happily, even in the midst of difficulties,
Of holding out my hand, even when utterly alone and
abandoned,
Of drying my tears, even while I weep,
Of believing, even when no one believes in me.

I have lived a lot of my life with a closed door and the wrong aspirations; it's not what we take from life but what we give. Most of the really rich people I've known are desperately unhappy with distorted expectations. Love, simplicity and tolerance are all values which constantly elude us.

We have to change society. People should be encouraged to spend their time on worthwhile community projects. We need to totally re-think our social services and give people meaningful work even if they're on benefits. Loss of self-esteem is a great cause of anguish within our society. When people ask 'why', I'm apt to say 'why not'? Be not afraid of the challenge, the Lord is with you. Break the barriers, express your feelings and do not be cowered into submission. The more I've been drawn into the spiritual side of life the more I've been made aware of the Machiavellian politics within the church, whether it is closing the school and shop at Buckfast with no community discussion, or attempting to move a well-loved priest at Medjugordje. The ego and the attraction of power overrides the spirit. Few have the ability to stand up for what is right and most of us would rather concur and have an easy life.

We seem to forget the example set by Jesus when it is convenient. It is staggering that so much division is still so prevalent with the established churches, whether it's the effect of the Fourth Crusade in the 11th century, which still rankles between the Greek Orthodox and the Roman church, or the situation in Northern Ireland. When, if ever, will man say there has been enough conflict, we must heal the world and live in peace?

Apathy prevails, most want a quiet, stable, regular routine whether it's watching *Coronation Street* or listening to *The Archers* omnibus every Sunday. We are obsessed with the outer being, rather than the inner self.

TO INDIA – AND SAI BABA

I arrived in Bombay from New Delhi knowing that I was supposed to go to Puttaparthi. I was told by the airline counter assistant that Sai Baba had cancelled flights to Puttaparthi and wanted me to fly to Bangalore. How, I thought, could anybody have the power to change the destination of an airline? At the baggage claim in Bangalore I met two German ladies, Marianne and Margaret, both of whom were frequent visitors to India and became my unofficial guides. George, Margaret's regular taxi driver, was found amongst the late night crowd and took us in his ancient diesel taxi, which he claimed he had owned since before the British left Whitefield in Bangalore. (Whitefield is a small town near Bangalore, which is the hi-tech, silicon valley of India).

Hotel rooms were hard to come by but Margaret, in her endearing Teutonic, way managed to secure three across the road from the Ashram. I was shown to my room and had to smile as there was only an iron bedstead and mattress and a solitary light bulb swaying in the middle of the room. I asked 'mine host' what I should do for a towel, toilet paper and sheets and he directed me to the market. It was quite a change from the Intercontinental in New Delhi.

The following day I was up and queuing to enter the Ashram at 5.30am and had to sit in a line until we were called to enter. I was amongst the first and sat close to the podium, cross-legged, whilst we waited. I had nothing to sit on apart from an inflatable neck support, not the most stable item on which to perch for an hour. Men and women were strictly divided for Darshan and I couldn't help but note the way the women ran to occupy what I presumed to be prized spots. Sai Baba entered at a great distance and there was a reverential hush. He was much smaller than I imagined and walked with a difficulty. He spoke to various people along the way and people passed him letters. In time, he passed close to me and I was aware of the power of his eyes and gaze; it cut one to the core. I hadn't brought a letter to give him and felt slightly out of place.

After Darshan I met my German guides to seek some hint as to what was going on and was told that the devotees brought letters with their various requests. Margaret was intriguing in that she was being guided by the angels to write a medical book with eight others in Germany and eventually gave me a leaving present, some *vibhuti*, or sacred ash, from Baba. Marianne had been given a ring which Baba had produced from nowhere. They were both guides sent to me by Baba to show me the way and help me along my path. Queuing between 5.30am and 6am is not my favourite pastime, though once one is in the rhythm it gets easier. I will always remember seeing a typical 'Annabel and Henry' who had obviously left their Range Rover at the airport. I was gobsmacked to see them later at a small lunch restaurant with about eight street kids having a pizza and cake, and that really brought home the need not to be judgmental.

Our wealth is within and it brings sheer joy when we attempt to trap it. My first experience with Baba was profound. I genuinely did not know what to expect so the road was full of enlightening discoveries. One is aware of a spiritual quest in all societies. So why Baba? It is his appeal for universal tolerance, love and compassion for all, whatever race, creed, culture or class. For once I'd found something which appealed to my own pragmatic view of life. I know that I have to work at it as in my heart I am full of prejudices and feelings of superiority and yet... we are all one.

My second visit to Baba was initially full of obstacles. I had booked my flight for 5 December, then on reflection tried to change it to 8 December; this was difficult and would mean paying a 50 per cent surcharge. I had great conflict in my soul whether to go or not...was it right? Was it wrong? I boarded the plane, and took my aisle seat next to an Indian lady who did not want to sit between two men. Her place was taken by a very large chap who wedged himself into the seat, left me no arm room and throughout the flight raised his arms, scratched his crotch, revealing doubtful personal hygiene.

I landed in Mumbai and spent the next 48 hours justifying my existence in India, visiting agents and the British Council. I left for Bangalore on Saturday wondering whether George, my friendly taxi driver from last year, would be there. On arrival I asked at the airport desk but they didn't know of George's whereabouts so I booked a taxi to Puttaparthi, three-and-a-half hours away, where Sai Baba was located. I left the airport and who should be standing there but George! We recognised one another instantly. I cancelled my original booking and got into George's rather elderly diesel Wolsey and embarked on another voyage of discovery. We got out of Bangalore by about one o'clock, when suddenly there was an amazing smell of diesel. Fortunately George pulled over as the fuel pipe had broken. It always amazes me where people appear from in India. One man materialised from a tyre shop, another with a fuel pipe - Indian self-help AA. We were soon on our way. George said he knew of a hotel, the Sai Renaissance, and proceeded to take me to it. It was quiet, exceedingly clean with sheets on the bed, towels and soap and loo paper in the bathroom, what treasures! I was soon ensconced and into the rhythm of rising at 5.30am for Darshan at 6.30am and back for breakfast and shower at eight.

On the first day there I got into conversation at breakfast with a woman named Donna. She was an exceedingly unusual woman and she offered to show me Puttaparthi that afternoon. At first I was taken aback as she spoke in terms of the being able to act as a channel not only for Sai Baba but also the universal powers. Initial scepticism gave way to the feeling that Sai Baba had placed me next to a steamroller. She led me up and down a path of self-discovery. I was challenged, past lives were explained from my being a king to helping the poor and even being nailed to a cross in the time of Jesus! A staggering amount of information was given to me and it was almost overload. She could answer my questions before I'd asked them. We visited the shrines at the hospitals, a Hindu temple in the middle of a lake, Sai Baba's grotto and the stadium. An excursion of one-and-a-half days turned into a series of mini-trips, all fascinating and revealing.

Donna had at one stage spent four to five years in a room in Puttaparthi, developing her inner-self and it made me realise how far along the path I still have to travel. There are certain people who are endowed with the ability to assume an earthly presence while being all-seeing. I had never met anybody like Donna before.

On my second day in Puttaparthi I met Marianne again, quite by chance and then took her for lunch every other day to a different restaurant. She's retired and lives on a meagre income. She was in reasonable spirits though this changed towards the end of the week when her hair began to fall out in clumps and she had to decide whether to return to Germany or stay in Puttaparthi and change her flights.

I bumped into Bob, a Kiwi, at the German bakery. He'd been coming to Sai Baba for three years, was retired and lived on a boat near Russell in the Bay of Islands, New Zealand. His story, like Donna's, was one of continual personal abuse as a child; he'd been to hell and back with the demon drink and then became a Jehovah's Witness for 28 years. Bob became my dinner chum and we discussed a wide range of issues. He was a good bloke and had interesting stories to tell of experiences with Sai Baba. He was another guide along life's rich river and pointed me in a number of directions. I was left with the distinct feeling that I have a mission in this life yet to be fulfilled but I am sure that every experience to date will be of some inherent value and it may tie into establishing schools for Sai Baba, an education first throughout the world to help spread love and compassion and create a universal consciousness.

FINDING MURTHY

This was when I was told about a palm reader by the German doctor and was determined to see him during my visit to Sai Baba. I rang and asked to see him on 19 December; he said he could only see me on the 21st, so I changed my flights. When I rang back he said that he was now able to see me on the 19th. According to Indian tradition everybody's palm may be interpreted by a good reader who can tell you about its life and past lives.

As I described briefly in my introduction to this series of lifetime experiences, I found Murthy in Bangalore. He was seated in a small whitewashed room with an exposed light bulb dangling in the middle. After I told him my age he proceeded to tell me about my upbringing and my three children. Sophie, he said, would study psychology, Tui would become a doctor/healer and Ollie would become a businessman. He went on to say first daughter, Sophie, would have artistic energy and my second daughter, Tui came to me for spiritual reasons. My marriage had broken down though I would always maintain good communications with my ex-wife. Murthy said I had had a previous life in India as a follower of Shri Baba, learning ayurvedic medicine and meditation and had voyaged in China as a teacher of martial arts, as well as being in New Zealand and Egypt. I was born in England as a navigator and would travel the world for knowledge and writing and he encouraged me to 'write small books'.

It is incredible what one can be told from a long piece of palm leaf. Murthy had never met me before and knew nothing about me; he traced my past lives to being one of the robbers crucified on the cross with Jesus, such startling stuff! Prone to hypertension, I needed to take up yoga, walking and eating slowly!

My chant:

Om Bhagavathe (phonetically spelt)
Holy Lord
    Dakshina Murthaye
    Shiva is in the form of intuition
Namaha
Surrending soul

Sai Baba - Oneness, Unity; there has to be a new spirituality developed within our society in order for it to survive. There is one God who can't be held responsible for all the love and hate in the world, we have to step outside existing boundaries and learn to love one another, whatever race, caste or religion we are from. It is a great joy to be in Puttaparthi for the festival of Divali, a time of light, joy and celebration, and then being hit by the media with news that Yasser Arafat has died, accused by a member of Israel's government as the source of terrorism. Explain that to the Palestinian parents who have lost loved ones. I'm sure that God is with us but we have to learn to see him in the eyes of our so-called enemies. Mandela taught the world a great lesson and we must seize upon it.

I had returned to Tondy Wood, my simple lodging at Whitefields near Bangalore. Now I am ensconced in an upgraded room with fan, just returned from Darshan, always an uplifting and interesting experience as many of the Indian devotees strive to get as close to the front as possible and thoughts come and go through one's monkey brain. It is wonderful to be grounded in the early morning and have the chance to ponder and question the meaning of life. There has to be far more tolerance and understanding and a commitment to saving our limited resources on earth; we must rise above our own self-interest and the illusion of material contentment. I look at many of my contemporaries, buying holiday homes in France, playing golf twice a week, in questionable relationships and wonder how you really feel when you're filling in time before the hereafter…. what's the point? Do we leave the world a better place? I doubt it.

I had to hire a car and driver to get there; the man drove like a maniac till I told him to slow down as I would prefer to see some of the scenery rather than end up in the back of a bus. As it was Remembrance Day I wore my poppy and had decided that I would stop him wherever we were at 11 minutes past 11 on the 11th day and say a few prayers for those who had fallen and were falling in present day conflicts. At 11.10 I got him to stop. I got out the car by the side of the road and there before me in the field was a large building with a white cross painted on it. Sometimes the unexpected in life is exceedingly powerful and this building and cross brought to mind the font overflowing with stars appearing and disappearing through a gap in the clouds which I'd seen whilst praying in a church on the Camino in Spain. I am sure that we live in a world of brick walls, and it's only when we break them down that we really see the light of our existence. God is light and love and there has to be a new tolerant world order where we rejoice and pray together and blame ourselves rather than God.

Puttaparthi was the centre for Sai Baba's main ashram whilst he was alive. It has a great energy of its own, though I'm always staggered in places of great worship that many of the people exude sorrow rather than joy. It does attract a lot of troubled people and perhaps we are all troubled and show it in different ways; we so rarely stop in our lives, take the foot off the pedal and just be. My path has been hazardous, as are most paths, but I'm exceedingly grateful for the privilege and joy of having Woodsie (Penny), my first wife from whom I'm amicably divorced. She has given me so much in that she's allowed me to walk my spiritual path unhindered as I attempt to find my true self. She allowed me to walk my spiritual path unhindered, together with Liz my long suffering partner who has journeyed with me over the years.

WHO DEFINES MORALITY?

It is a hot muggy evening in Puttaparthi. Diwali in full swing; an amazing festival, it makes Chinese New Year look tame, just like the battle of Fallujah, crackers, bangs, smoke everywhere, the whole place is a cacophony of noise. I usually walk everywhere but not tonight. Sai has a policy of not giving money to beggars so I bought milk powder for the leper who has been following me and set off by *tuk tuk* (a local motorbike taxi). I had tea with a German woman who had been here for a year doing puja and healing the world. She felt that Sai had a sugar problem and so he wasn't enjoying anything! She decided that she would stay here for good. It takes all sorts! And a Dutch woman who had spent three weeks with the Dalai Lama and was here until the 20th, extremely proud that Sai had sent her a grandchild, which didn't say much for her son or daughter.

India is a bit like Africa - Kenya to be precise - where American tourists go into the shop next to the Norfolk Hotel, and come out dressed like something 'out of Africa'; here, it's looking like Gandhi and putting a painted spot on your forehead. I guess it's whatever turns you on. I always remember reading about split spirituality where we are able to hear the world, compute it and not live it; we're all self-absorbed to a greater or lesser degree, we do need to walk our talk, overcome our prejudices and learn to love one another. I found it bloody hard being true to oneself and totally truthful. Convention forces conformity, conditioning is accepted by most, a routine is all important, success is measured outwardly not inwardly, and we are fed a daily dose of power and dominance through the media. We waste billions on arms when so many need clean water and the means to overcome the effects of diarrhoea. The Roman Catholic Church bans the use of condoms even amidst a population explosion and the frightening spread of Aids. We must improve beyond our present position or our world as we know it will implode. Communities based on self-respect and the family need to be re-established; far too many communities are subject to fear, youths are alienated and yobbishness prevails. It is interesting looking at Britain: if our Asian and Muslim youth feels as many other youths do, we must be creating a feeding ground for more terrorists and even furthering the spread of Jihad. Not only do individuals have to stop and listen but also nations need to take a similar course. Who defines morality, what is right or wrong, which course of action would heal? Love all, serve all.

I had just finished reading *Tomorrow's God* which was awe-inspiring and reinforced my view that as humanity we need to find another way. In essence we are all one and most religious groups claim ownership of God rather than accepting that they have their path and other paths are equally as valid. Religion for many youngsters is boring and uninspiring with no relevance in their eyes. There is a lack of realisation that the godhead is within us all; enlightenment to me is each individual finding his or her own spiritual path - we don't need to belong to a fashionable group and be led like sheep. All the answers that we need are within us. Love and joy are paramount. We've all been conditioned by an educational process which to many seems like an exam conveyor belt; we are not inspiring youngsters to create, we teach, they learn, it is rarely a two-way process. All of my kids are far superior to me in the use of the DVD and what you can do with a mobile phone and computer. I'm still in the dark ages and in their eyes have fond memories of quill pens.

Many people worldwide are restless, dissatisfied with their political rules and searching for a more meaningful existence. We are taught to consume, accumulate and not share. The Englishman's home is his castle and beware anyone who crosses the ramparts. Many people within the UK are innately racist, but it's not a subject we talk about; now, however, there is a realisation that we have a lot to learn from our Indian community about family values. I saw a wonderful film recently, *Wondrous Oblivion*, about a West Indian family who moved in next to a Jewish family and the various conflicts and joys that they went through before a true understanding emerged. We are who we are, we must listen to our hearts and be honest within ourselves. Once we've climbed one mountain, we must be prepared for the next.

There are many masters, just as there are many prophets. Listen, read, be tolerant of others who take a different path. An afterthought: the environment can be very stressful. Many of the poorer Indians can't seem to relax, having to constantly move and shove, there is great urgency in their actions. The ashram is run like the Indian Civil Service, a lot of power entrusted to a few and plenty of young go-fers with too much ego and not enough spirit, perhaps. I came away with the very strong sense that the world must change; we cannot continue to finance a navy, air force and army and also have people in shackles without running water or other essentials for peaceful cohabitation. Reconciliation, re-creation and reflection - these are three R's with so much hidden power. It always staggers me how young women and the not so young in countries like India and Thailand can sit surrounded by absolute filth and crap and yet look so demure and exquisitely beautiful.

I realised that Sai is with you everywhere. It was great to reconnect but I am aware of his presence in my being. I learnt something this morning at Darshan: it's New Year's Day for Gujarat, following Diwali and Eid, and it's been an action-packed few days, the celebration of life and life force.

MEDJUGORDJE – A SHINING LIGHT

This is a town in the Herzegovina region of Bosnia, close to the border of Croatia. Since 1981 it has become a popular site for Catholic pilgrimage following reports of apparitions of the Virgin Mary to six local Catholics.

One is instantly struck by the peace and the affluence of the locals as you get off the bus from the airport. Initially I was perplexed to be sitting with a group of pilgrims chanting The

Angelus and hearing about the good deeds of 'Our Lady' but the experience was and is angelic. My guide for my first visit was Father Pat, a likeable Irish priest who swiftly changed into a Hawaiian suit and sandals and found sustenance in a gin and tonic. The group at Santa Maria's House were quite elderly, good and devout, with the outspoken Nora, sharing local knowledge on who was doing what and where.

The place has a calmness and tranquillity and one cannot help but be touched inwardly. There is a definite presence of energy in the environment. I find it staggering that the visionaries had their first experience of 'Our Lady' in 1981 - people disbelieved them and they were hauled off on numerous occasions by the local police to see if they were of sound mind. The local parish priest was even imprisoned for 18 months because after initial disbelief he heard a voice in his parish church and supported the visionaries.

The bishop was, and is, non-supportive of the visionaries. A new bishop who has been installed takes a similar view, much to the chagrin of many pilgrims. It really is like a scenario from the Middle Ages with Dominicans who oversee the shrine at loggerheads with the bishop who is known to shout and berate clergy. One lady wishes to build a housing block for the sick and elderly who at present are moved, in some cases, to Sarajevo. She has the financial backing and support from the government but the bishop is unwilling to give his approval. Medjugordje is a shining light in the midst of the place where most atrocities since the Second World War were committed. It is very much a light in the darkness, surrounded as it is by Mostar and Srebrenica where some of the worst atrocities of the Bosnian war occurred. The situation in Mostar in uneasy and the slaughter of Muslim men in Srebrenica still hangs in the mind.

But now, I have never seen so many Mercedes and BMWs in one small area, even the photo shop man has a Mercedes 350SL. The shops within the town are generally run by sultry, indifferent young ladies to whom service is anathema and prices vary considerably from one end of the shopping street to the other. Most of the religious junk on offer finds a market amongst the busloads of pilgrims. It's a bit like being in Greece - most of the shops are selling identical tat.

MY 'LIFE'S GUIDES'

My companion on this visit to the Balkans was Father Ghirma, an Ethiopian priest who was looking after refugees in London. He'd been in Europe for a few months and had turned up virtually unexpectedly, spending 15 days wandering the streets of London. The bishop in Medjugordje was not expecting him and his primary purpose was to study, which he had to curtail.

Life throws up a number of guides - what pleasure they bring. Another was the Very Reverend Reg Pellant, a former RAF chaplain and Queen's chaplain, who opened up the spiritual world for me and made me think inwardly and question – it was an amazing voyage driven by curiosity and perhaps a call from on high to see and experience. We have to listen to our hearts and as Sai Baba so rightly says: "Serve all and love all", and awaken the godhead in each and every one of us.

It never ceases to surprise me that there is very little apparent joy in a number of 'charged' places. People, generally are apt to look incredibly worried as though they are carrying the troubles of the world on their shoulders. With some people, whatever is told to them seems to have a superficial impact. I remember one Australian lady (a good Catholic) who felt that the Australian prime minister

135

could not apologise to the Aboriginal people because it would open up a number of court cases. The Aborigines, as we all know, were driven off their lands and hunted for sport like animals. When will people realise that there must be a spirit of reconciliation? Wherever there is light there is also darkness and I genuinely believe that we have to be aware of the forces of darkness. Man seems to live in vicious circle of power, greed and ego and it will take a great statesman to break that cycle. Most religions preach tolerance and compassion though it is not always apparent.

I have found Sai Baba's message most profound and will always remember the two German ladies that he sent to me as guides. The contrast between staying in a five star hotel in Delhi and a room opposite the ashram in Bangalore will stay with me forever. A bed, mattress and light bulb, but such joy even though I was unused to sitting on a concrete floor for hours and unaware that most people write him letters with requests.

We must awaken to the need to give children a spiritual education - but in what sort of framework? Who monitors and assesses? I felt that it was lovingly disorganised and there was very little idea what was happening from one day to the next; it took the word 'unstructured' to the limits. I just feel it needs to be placed on a more professional, transparent structure.

THE POLITICS OF BARCHESTER

Nothing so masks the face of God as religion. How very true; there is so much bigotry, dogma, ego and pride amongst mankind. Many need to wear a label 'I'm a born again Christian' or the Bible says such and such. It has always confounded me that the Bible can be interpreted in so many ways and has been used throughout history to justify incredible misdeeds. The Anglican

Church at present is being torn apart by the homosexual debate and yet a great part of the Anglo Catholic Church is camp. As I discovered at Walsingham, in certain colleges it was the custom to be known by your mother's Christian name. One is left with the vision of any number of Maureens and Gladys's meeting at services. I have had the fortune to live within the confines of an English cathedral where Trollopian politics (yes, of *Barchester Towers*) prevail and one is constantly reminded of the Machiavellian intrigue which is second to none and the hierarchy is seemingly more concerned with the fact that they all have doctorates than the spiritual high that they foster in the community.

Sunday morning communion at 8.15 is regularly attended by what Gerard Hughes would perhaps call 'the frozen people'. People lose themselves in the choir stalls, rarely acknowledge one another and are rarely met by a priest on leaving the service. One classic remark was by someone who spoke on class and said that he'd overcome the class problem in his parish in Barnes by having one verger who was a public school master and another who was a gardener and they spoke to one another! Whoopy do! I nearly wrote to the Bishop wondering in which world this man existed: sadly for him he has a 'freehold' living at the cathedral until he's 68. The Anglican church 'purse' is divided, bigoted and seemingly ego-driven. A 'here' rather than 'there' attitude prevails. Even in a small cathedral city the church seems detached from the realities within the community of yobbishness and juvenile delinquency.

There is hope and that hope comes from the Ionas of the world, and from Lourdes which, although on the exterior it comes across as a religious 'Woolworths' run by the 'Ave Maria' society, it is inspiring to see the elderly and sick being cared for by the young. The spirit is alive and kicking, it just needs to be drawn open. Become who you are, be inspired, go to the edge of the cliff and fly. God is within us but we need to find that special place in life, that moment to really connect and have the guts to genuinely express our views. Much frustration, I am sure, emanates from the fact that many of us spend our lives trying to create the right impression or say the right thing; our social status and self-esteem are all important and beware anybody who questions or criticises us. It takes balls and courage to go into the unknown, but we have to do it.

The analogy within the Church is that we are like sheep and the priest is the shepherd of the flock and conformity abounds. Whether it be the Dean in the cathedral or the headmaster in the school, they seem to profess this god given right to always be right. Beware the person who challenges or criticises us: 'Thou shalt not last'. Power corrupts and it is just as prevalent inside the Church as it is in the secular world.

Any failure can become a moment of grace - these words that ring true in our lives however many rocks have been thrown across our paths. The trouble is that most people only appreciate the transformation that's taken place in retrospect. As I described earlier, I spent ten years of my life building up a chain of schools in Australia and New Zealand. There were four schools and all was before me, as I had the financial backing of one of the longest running travel and tour operators in New Zealand. I did it all on a shoestring, ploughed in all my available cash and all seemed rosy until the crash of '87. The travel company was taken over, the buyer sold off all its assets on the open market, including peripheral assets and subsidiaries. I was left owning four schools with money seeping away as though I was a colander. I didn't listen to my own intuition and my inner being to heed the warning that pride goes before a fall.

I turned to a friend in the educational industry, a well-known Irish businessman with the reputation of a likeable rogue, with his personalised number plates and ostentatious gold jewellery. He sent his accountant to New Zealand and did his 'due diligence' and then returned again later in the year to do further due diligence. My back was to the wall and they took a controlling interest of 51 per cent in September, being well aware of my situation. On 6 December the Irishman phoned me and told me to close the schools in Brisbane and Sydney on the following day. I pleaded to keep the school open until Christmas but to no avail. He said that his board were not concerned about students being turned away the following day, although most of them were Swiss, as this wouldn't impinge on their international reputation. I returned to New Zealand and arranged a merger for the Sydney school but it wasn't to be. It all tumbled like a pack of cards and quite understandably I was made the scapegoat.

Worse was to come. The Irish investor, as MD, decided to keep the NZ schools open and hold me to my 'service' contract. At that point in my life I had no money, no support and had no control over events. He chose to go ahead with a successful asset strip as both NZ schools were financially viable, Brisbane was breaking even and Sydney was a loss-maker. I felt desperate, lonely, humiliated, the roof had caved in. I experienced three years of anger and resentment and got to my lowest ebb, not knowing which way to turn - I had to work for, and be in contact with, somebody who made all his actions seem plausible. I had to admit that I'd been wrong, taken crass decisions and forgive him as he had, in my eyes, been solely guided by mammon.

Sometime later, the Irishman was appointed as Managing Director of a very large educational company in the UK, turning failing schools and colleges around. The irony is that the company also re-established the schools in Australia.

This experience was tough and yet character-building because my inner godhead gave me strength and the will to rise again, phoenix-like, wiser and better balanced. Occasionally in our lives we are driven to periods of what T. S. Elliot would call 'quiet desperation'. Who am I, what am I, who can I turn to - many are led to the mystery of Christ. It is a funny old world - this moment of failure became a moment of grace. Generosity, compassion and goodness have to prevail, we must move away from being inspired just for our own self-interest.

The Iona community is one which embodies all the afore-mentioned qualities and one can't help but be touched by the spirituality of the services and the power of the words used. It's a wonderful blend of young and old, and togetherness and sense of community. Anybody, however, can afford to stay on the island, there are no barriers and genuine compassion prevails.

RELIGIOUS BUT NOT SPIRITUAL

On my walk through life, it is a surprise to discover how many people one comes across in reasonably 'holy' settings who seem to live in a world of self-deception and use God and Christ to justify their own way of thinking, whether it be Ian Paisley or an evangelical Anglican. They are religious and not spiritual; spirituality comes from within, the result of recognition, realisation and reverence - the three R's. How can I give? What can I give? Most live in a quandary in choppy, unchartered waters; if only we could find the restful bay and appreciate the power of silence.

Make me an instrument of your peace.
Walk your talk. Strut your stuff.

One of the most inspirational books I've read is *Siddhartha* by Herman Hesse. In essence, its message is that our life is a river voyage and when we jump into a river we are apt to cling to the logs

140

at the side because they stop us from drowning but as soon as we learn to let go we are carried by the current and ride the rapids of life and sometimes become calmed in the still waters. After the breakdown of my marriage I let go and started an interesting and fascinating illuminating journey, guided in a way I never thought imaginable. I am sure that we are guided and people point us in certain directions if only we'd listen. We are so concerned with our own inner worries and what we can take from life that we've lost the art of being still and listening to our heartbeat; we need to be grounded and free to give ourselves. Life is a rich tapestry of experience and we all live the fear of not being loved, not having enough money and loneliness.

As Sai Baba so rightly says:

There is only one caste, the caste of humanity
There is only one language, the language of the heart
There is only one religion, the religion of the Love
There is only one God, He is omnipresent

I remember being interviewed for reader training in the Anglican church and, being asked what I would preach on, I suggested love or tolerance. The woman interviewing asked me to give biblical references relating to tolerance. I knew then we were on different paths and I said, look around you in the world today. Has it really changed from biblical times? Why must everything have a reference? Love and speak as you see it. The bishop then asked me what was my view of God and it reminded me of the stoics – "In him I live and move and have my being". I am aware God has great humour and I was then asked to write about uncleanliness in Leviticus and how it applied to women and what was the modern church's view to uncleanliness. I thought, I'm in the wrong place, at the wrong time and my spiritual path should be heading elsewhere.

I have often regretted having spoken, but never of having been silent (to quote Abba Arsenius). I've always admired the Quakers being moved by the spirit and valuing the power of silence. How often do many of us really stop and listen? At Buckfast, I sat with Father Sebastian after compline recently; he sat on a bench in the grounds of the abbey and said nothing. After a while he turned and said he could really appreciate the power of the silence at this time of the evening.

I've frequently stopped on a walk, especially in Germany, and listened to the sounds of nature - we're frequently in such a great rush we're never really grounded throughout the day, we've lost the rhythm of the seasons both in the way we live and what we eat, we import food from afar and do not eat what is in season. Our knowledge of the countryside, especially amongst the young, is very limited; ask the average person to name a tree, flower or bird and he or she would be struggling to answer. Society in many ways is becoming emasculated while many people live in fear, especially the elderly, of being mugged, burgled or assaulted. Communities are fragmented, family is an illusion for so many, and gangs of unruly youth seem to cast mayhem in many smaller towns.

PEACE AND SILENCE

Iona is a spectre'd isle off the coast of Mull, a special place full of wonderful energies, whatever one reads or dreams in life, Iona brings home the sense of balance and harmony that is required to fulfil our real sense of purpose in this world. Listening to the sounds of nature, the birds, the sea, the wind, reinforces the fact that many of us have lost contact with the elements, with mother nature, as we become increasingly driven by mass consumerism and the stresses and strains of modern life. Whatever spiritual or new age one reads and follows, whether it be White Eagle or a course in kinesiology, for example, they all stress the need for balance and harmony between the emotional, physical, spiritual and mental aspects within us, and until we re-connect with the natural world this will never really happen. Many are totally out of cycle with it; gardening is spurned in most schools, most people have an exceedingly limited knowledge of the flowers, insects and trees around us. How much better would we be if we ate vegetables that were in season and not imported from some far off land?

The community of Iona brings home the fact in its own subtle way that we have lost our own sense of community. The family, nuclear and extended, is frayed at the edges and failing as a high proportion of our children rarely even get to know two parents.

Many people are beginning to look inwards and seek another path - the inner light shines, we let our inner selves shine and this casts away the anxieties, fears and stresses that shroud us, and helps us to rediscover ourselves. I am very wary of labels and find people who introduce themselves as 'born again' Christians quite scary; we've all sinned, Christ has always been there, God is within us and we are all part of his wonderful creation.

Iona... the peace, the mist, the silence, that wonderful gift when you know you are in the presence of the Father, our life force. We long for silence away from the noise and hustle; it provides clarity to our thoughts and our very being. We are all searching along life's rich path but we are apt to look outwards rather than inwards at our flawed selves and should be attempting to create a caring, compassionate world guided by love towards one another. There is tremendous power and energy within yet we fail to tap the source. Acceptance of who we are and where we are is half the battle. On Iona we can visit Angel's Mount and thank our guardian angels for watching over us and amble over to St Columbia's beach

143

where legend has it that one can throw a stone into the water and caste away one's troubles. Faith moves mountains, the power of the spirit soars, we must get back to basics. It is important that we all seek a spiritual path; wherever that may lead it will certainly bring tremendous joy and the inner peace and equilibrium that we all strive for.

Yes, Iona is a special place; there's a certain energy and feeling that draws one back like a magnet. The gentle waves, the seagulls, the solitude, the amazing community spirit which exudes from the abbey, one feels one's load being lifted. We all have a need to be re-charged and re-focused and this is one place where that can happen. One has an appreciation for one's offspring and all we can hope is that they pursue a spiritual path at some point in their lives - they may not find answers but they will find an inner peace and appreciate that God moves in a mysterious way. Our guides are forever those people we must listen to, change direction at times and break open the cages that incarcerate us.

On Iona people acknowledge you, have the time to talk and tolerance and love abound. The community services are normally 'youth' led and full of the magic and vitality of the spiritual world. This is my third visit and the first time that I've stayed at a retreat house rather than a hotel and if I ever had to write a TV comedy 'next to heaven' this would be the place; it's full of elderly Episcopalian Scots, who have been coming every year since Adam was a boy scout, and an evangelical group from North London. One poor lady told me she had been scorned and spurned by the church because she successfully practised homeopathy. Where on earth has our tolerance disappeared to? I was pleasantly interrogated by one old drunk as to whether the kinesiology course I run at Buckfast was Christian based... I had visions of giving everyone a name tag. 'I am Peter and I am a Christian', as though it makes any difference at all - the house of God to me is full of many doors and it doesn't matter which one you enter, as long as you enter one and find your own path. The end of another path or perhaps the beginning of a voyage with the angels. We're apt to be sceptical about them in our everyday lives, though I'm quite sure that we have a guardian angel looking over us - and why shouldn't there be angels looking over every part of our world? Because we can't see it, we shouldn't knock it. A dog can hear sounds a human ear can't, why shouldn't some people see things that other can't? I've tried bloody hard to connect with the inner world but it doesn't seem to want to happen.

A VISIT TO GOA

It was an intriguing experience to visit El Shaddai (a children's charity housing and teaching homeless children) in Goa. There was no Matthew at the airport to meet me. I hung around from 2.30pm to 3.30pm to no avail. I knew the name of the hotel, the Colonial Braganza, and I had an address for El Shaddai in Mapusa. But Matthew's mobile number was answered by somebody who had recently returned from Kuwait and all of the office numbers were disconnected. I hired an air-con taxi and took off for Mapusa, but nobody there had any knowledge of the Colonial Braganza - not a great start. Fortunately, I wasn't a volunteer arriving. I had my credit cards and the ability to stay anywhere. We found a hotel in Mapuso called the Braganza. Yes, they said, there was a Colonial Braganza but it was in Calangute - onward Christian soldiers!

The room was at least clean and there was hot water and a small pool surrounded by obese, shaven-headed 'Poms' with tattooed arms watching large screen football. I found Sharon who told me these Poms were staying in the hotel and that we were all going to church on the Sunday. Alan and Jean were charming, gruff northerners from Rochdale. He looked troubled initially and happened not to be a happy chappie, particularly with the hotel which they had had to endure for three weeks. At once, I saw that the place had a charming decadence about it. On Sunday, the faith community service started with a group of musicians playing. We sang and sang for the first hour, then there were many testimonies and prayers and the service finished within three hours. The joy of the spirit was there and it was quite moving, apart from the odd disruption of a woman behind me mumbling loudly in the aisle. I agreed to re-connect with Anita in the evening and took her for dinner at the beach. She certainly loves the children and has had an interesting life with her first husband (now on his sixth marriage) and her second husband was jailed for abuse with her two daughters; therein lies a tale. Her mind is like a scatter-gun, throwing out ideas and thoughts at great rapidity and her drawback could be that she asks a number of people to undertake the same tasks. Matthew turned out to be an enthusiastic pastor, overly joyful but something just doesn't add up: the charity was looking after 17 children in 1997 and now cares for possibly 1,000 children in its homes and night shelters.

Great play is made of being a committed Christian, but it's only a label, especially when one considers the level of child abuse that the Catholic Church has had to face. I think that El Shaddai is troubled by the rapid expansion it has experienced. One can always say that it's the way things are done in India and mask it with the veil of our Lord - but we visited the very well-equipped upmarket head offices while the school had no books... this is troubling. I attended the school as guest of honour for children's day, a touching event with dances, songs and plays. It was a moving experience; they are all on the right path and love is paramount for the kids but without being cynical I was left with a feeling of unease. Why? Intuition? El Shaddai has had a chequered path to date and one can only wish it well as these children are being given a wonderful opportunity to live, though none of the teachers in the school are trained and the principal, even though she is loving and caring, has no qualifications or experience. However, I believe that things there have now changed for the better.

I've just read that the education authorities in UK want to introduce texting and surfing the net in English classes, as though watching soaps aren't enough. We must retain our knowledge of the classics – but I sound like my father, a voice in the wind.

I remember… Sai Baba calls, Mother Meera sends - I am sure they both want the world to be a better place where everyone attempts to follow a spiritual path at his or her own pace. You can have everything and yet nothing, how often does one hear that said by people searching, who have everything in a material sense? Seek humility, do good, look inside and discover but don't become self-obsessed to the detriment of humanity... I'm all right but bollocks to everybody else!

EL CAMINO DE SANTIAGO

"The Camino was born from the faith of our ancestors, who were seeking something; the clear aim of faith is to express our inner selves, the life within us. Logically, the Camino expresses the faith within us. They complement each other in the Camino. We are speaking about the culture of the Camino of Santiago, which is an expression of the faith."

I have walked the Camino, or parts of it, many times over the years. So what is the Camino? Trekking, tourism? I can't deny that some pilgrims may begin the Camino without knowing what they are doing, some to know themselves, others to get to know Jesus Christ. Logically, trekking and tourism are not the only things

147

tied to the Camino of Santiago. It can be enjoyed but the Camino is not designed as a vacation. Although a human being can think on vacation, on the Camino we have always to adopt an attitude of searching.

On the way with David, left.

The wonderful thing about walking is that it's a great leveller and you can be as sociable as you wish to be or walk alone. I always remember seeing a rather forlorn young lady in our first year who seemed extremely downtrodden when we started but had flowered by the end of the week. The Camino has transformed many lives and given people the opportunity to get their ducks in a row. To me the Camino is:

UNIVERSALITY: The Camino is universal without exclusive identities. We all feel as one and each traveller experiences a small universe.

148

FRATERNITY: You can find brotherhood through shared vision, projects, plans, you can live amongst equal others.

It is an interior way of knowing oneself, being capable of discovering the capacity that we have of sharing ourselves with others.

It is about searching and meeting: searching oneself, because sometimes we are strangers to ourselves and some can find Jesus Christ.

It is also a time to consider our values which can be lost in the trials and rush of life.

It is to take on realistic and feasible projects and not to feel overwhelmed by life.

It is for believers in love, not for people who fear or dread.

It is to be a witness of Christ and to give Jesus' testimony to others and to give our walk to Jesus.

It is a time to see our mistakes and to overcome them, to see our successes and to celebrate.

Everything is possible in life. We should be free in the Camino, free from guilt, and more forward.

Don't be afraid to live life, go forward! Christ waits for you with opened arms. He needs us to change this world individually.

GOOD CAMINO!

From an 8am departure, we are following a cycle route, initially straight uphill. It is well signposted, the yellow arrows are in a remarkably good state of repair considering the passing of 50,000 pilgrims per year. There is a diversity of scenery, recalling parts of the Peak District and Yorkshire Dales and Australia, but with eucalyptus trees and a lack of sheep and goats.

149

There is friendliness amongst pilgrims, who are predominantly Spanish, with little, if any, English spoken. We see interesting churches and villages and spend six to eight hours walking per day, with brief stops and lunch on arrival at 3pm or 4pm. David, my colleague, showed that there's still good life in a 65-year-old. He had done no training and kept up a cracking pace. A reasonable level of fitness is required. People of all ages are walking. Cyclists, predominantly young, aren't allowed into the refuges until all the walkers have arrived. They are regarded very much as second class citizens, though it is feasible for them to cycle St James' Way in two weeks!

We followed in the footsteps of a musical group from a small parish church near Valencia so each evening was enlivened by mass accompanied by guitars. The food offered was all cooked the same way and most meals consisted of a choice between meat or fish and chips, preceded by soup. It was all cooked in the same oil and was reasonably priced at £4-£5. Carrying a pack took some getting used to and I seem to be blessed with a pack containing everything apart from the kitchen sink.

The reasons for undertaking the walk are manifold but one can't help being touched by a certain prevailing spirituality. To re-earth ourselves and be touched by nature is something that we sorely miss in our modern society.

MARK'S PILGRIMAGE

Another of my companions was Mark Matthews - a healer, homeopath, osteopath and kinesiologist, a singular man, pleasantly eccentric with great passion and intellect. He has raised thousands of pounds through his own endeavours for the Sunflower Trust which helps children and adults who suffer from dyslexia and learning difficulties.

Here is his story.

Following in the footsteps of pilgrims to Santiago de Compostela:

This was certainly different to the mountains, forests and moors I am usually drawn to which allow me to commune with nature and refresh my mind and body with invigorating exercise and the chance to think uninhibited by the day-to-day of work and home. I was inspired to participate by Peter Harris, who had walked part of the route with his friend David last year, and was keen to enjoy a new kind of experience, a place I had not been to before with a chance to gain some sponsorship for the work of the Sunflower Trust.

Peter works for the King's School in Ely where he ensures that the English teaching annexe is always full of young people from all over the world, enjoying the benefits of an English education in a particularly beautiful and historic place. David took on the job of bursar for Ely Cathedral after retiring from his work in the food industry. He has all the dignified bearing of a man of the cloth. The fourth member of our little group of pilgrims was Liz. After a successful career editing and then managing provincial newspapers and working for BBC radio, she is now also working for King's School as marketing and media relations officer.

Having arrived in Bilbao, minus my rucksack, which only reached me on the third day, we motored down to Leon from where we were to begin our walk. Luckily I had my walking boots in a carrier bag, as they would not fit in the

151

rucksack! Then came the next problem - having worn sandals all summer I now found that my feet had spread and were reluctant to be squashed into the walking boots. It was a great relief when my luggage finally caught up with me, to be able to cut the side of my walking boots away with my Swiss army knife and take the pressure off my now lacerated toes. Fortunately we had no rain after that!

The route was very mixed, reflecting as it does the many sides of life. Even though my feet gave great pain for the first few days there were times when I did not notice, so engrossed was I in conversation with one or another of my companions or liberated by a beautiful view or fascinated by the historic architecture. As we followed the signs, clam shells or yellow arrows, through the towns, villages, hills and countryside we were connecting with the landscapes of history through to St. James, who had first visited these parts to preach the gospel. On his return to Jerusalem he was apprehended and beheaded. His followers took the Saint's remains to where Santiago now stands. Long forgotten, other than by folk memory, the tomb was rediscovered in the 9th century. The town of Compostela has been a place for pilgrims ever since.

On any one day, there were perhaps a few dozen people from, all over the world journeying over any part of the long route, which starts in France, all walking at their own pace for their own reasons; in the summer it could be over 1000. Some places were ancient, atmospheric and beautiful, others just old deserted ruins. On the outskirts of even the most wonderful old places were all the detritus of modern day living, rubbish dumps, scrap-yards, warehouses and electricity pylons. At times you could be walking through the woods and fields, moors and hill pastures, quite

152

reminiscent of parts of the Welsh border country, but at other times the trail led along hard roads, which were the worst on my sensitive feet.

Mark's holey boots.

David, Liz, Peter and Mark.

The 12th century castle at Ponferrada exceeded the expectation of any schoolboy fantasy of what a castle should be, with its ornate castle towers, drawbridges and maze of staircases and multi-level walkways and passages. It was the Knights Templars in their struggle against the advancement of the Moors in the Middle Ages, who fought to keep these communication routes open.

At the top of the highest mountain pass on the Camino a rustic monk rang a bell to welcome any passing pilgrims into his old stone dwelling to help themselves to coffee and biscuits and marvel at the kind of lifestyle, which reminded me of some of the hippy communes I visited in Wales in the 1960s and 1970s.

We tried to start walking reasonably early in the morning. It is a great way to be with people, sometimes on your own doing your own journey inside and outside, sometimes with companions or a stranger, exchanging pleasantries or indeed thoughtful conversation. There are many places on the way where you can get a coffee and get your notebook stamped as evidence of your pilgrim status. When we arrived at our designated hotel in the afternoon, there was time to wash, read, write or sleep and we would all meet up for a good meal together at 9 o'clock - a wonderful way to enjoy sharing time with my companions.

We four 'Peregrinos' (pilgrims) completed our walk at Santiago in the province of Galicia. Santiago itself is a fantastic place and the cathedral truly awesome in its size and ornate magnificence of architecture and intricate carvings of silver, gold and wood, depicting heaven itself on the inside.

The beautiful white clamshell is the emblem worn by peregrinos to identify themselves. They also relate to the fine cuisine supported by the important fisheries and shellfish beds, which are an integral part of the coastal ecology and economy.

We went back to Leon by train and returned to Bilbao by car, on a brand new motorway straddling the plains on the southern side of the green hills. It was like some part of the United States, miles of prairie, fields of maize but not a soul to be seen. You could drive for twenty minutes without even seeing another car.

One wonders why such massive expenditure was given to such an unnecessary infrastructure. On the upside, we reached Bilbao well ahead of schedule and had time to have a brief look at the Guggenheim Museum before booking in for our return flight. It is a massive outdoor modern sculpture of odd shapes, which contains within it a mass of offices, galleries and public spaces, clad in a kind of tin foil, which you can bend with your fingers. Like much modern architecture, I suspect that it will have disappeared long before the many wonderful old buildings we enjoyed on our journey.

MORE CAMINO MEMORIES

One year, my Camino started in Los Arcos with Geoff, Jill, Richard, Mark and David, which made me feel something like a tour operator rather than a *peregrinos*. We decided to send our bags ahead for the first two days as the distances to be covered were 27 kms and 28 kms. It was hot - shorts and t-shirt weather. The sun beat down and there was a certain relief in not carrying a pack. Emotions ebbed and flowed. People need the security of being told

155

what to do and when to do it rather than placing their faith in just being. The walk reflects and immerses all human emotions in a very short time; you can be happy, sad, maudlin, reflective but there is an overriding joy in just being and doing, sinking to the various depths of the mind and discovering your inner self. I regard the walk as a spiritual pilgrimage, others regard it just as a walk.

The accommodation varies from day-to-day but there is great joy in clean sheets, a warm shower and heating in the room! The 'menu peregrinos' is an excellent find, meals cost seven or ten euros and there is a plentiful supply of wine. Mass in the evening is a focal point and this year David celebrated mass, the Scottish Liturgy, in his room. It is wonderful in life to pose the question why are we here and what are we doing; in many areas our spiritual wells are dry as we are driven by a raging consumerism.

Many of the churches along the way were locked but one in particular was memorable. I was drawn to pray and before me I saw a font filled with white, it began to overflow and stars sparkled then it rose through a hole in the clouds to the heavens, it filled me with excitement and peace. Great spiritual joy possessed the body and the mind. This point of the Camino has given me a great especially inner awareness - I realise that I must trust, have faith and be guided by my inner self. One can buy books and guides and dispute distances but the security is within, all will be well, you never know what is around the corner.

Richard flourished on the Camino. He is a man of great learning, especially in things regarding Romans in Gaul. He was a good companion who really unwound whilst walking the Camino. I always remember him telling me his most enjoyable job was as a student lorry driver rather than as the headmaster of a prestigious school.

156

I try and instil in all my companions the idea that they must each treat the Camino in their own way. Jeff and Jill decided not to walk for a couple of days. Mark likes to leave early, everybody walks at his or her own pace, nothing is cast in stone. Stay in a *refugio* (a simple place of rest) if you wish to, but it's not for me. Walk and talk with others, be as you wish to be, but accept that the accommodation varies tremendously, as does the weather, and that our plans frequently change; accept all lovingly and be at peace. We are driven at certain stages in life to find our inner being, connect with our souls and shout, 'bugger it, this is me'. Convention moulds us, gives a certain sense of security but we must always question and be willing to accept that we've been wrong and shift the paradigm of our own being. Work flows, thoughts provoke, humanity leads us onwards. Perhaps life is one long pilgrimage or, for some, a circular route back to the security of childhood. Why must we always define and scientifically prove? Perhaps our lives should be in the mystical and rest in the joy of being or attaining that wonderful space between earth and heaven which is sometimes revealed or attained by listening to a choir or music in a cathedral or church or an individual singing *Pie Jesu* or *Ave Maria*.

Here, then, are some extracts from my notes on the six-day walk.

Day One

Hurricane Wilma greeted us! Our 7.10am flight has been delayed due to engine problems. We arrive in Bilbao at 1.30pm. The next bus is at 3.15pm. Fortunately we are in an excellent bus station for a Spanish lunch and eventually arrive in Burgos in drizzle followed by torrential rain. It was 7km to Villabella. My pack is too heavy, what should I have left at home? Mark strides away in sodden sandals. We meet

David and Richard who are in fine form. It feels good to be grounded.

Day two

We are met by an angelic lady in a nun's outfit handing out St Christopher's - touched by someone special; a long haul slog then stop at a bar resembling something from the middle ages with wooden jugs and ox yokes. The proprietor poured wine onto his forehead and let it run down his nose into his mouth, quite spectacular. Covered 32kms, feeling knackered but joyful. David's knee is playing up and we have a long way to go.

Day three

A long one, 25km with a rucksack, feeling very weary, but it's a great walk. A heart-tester out of town, followed by a wonderful easy walk. We nearly cause a riot at our lunch stop by taking olives from a bar which obviously somebody has paid for. We live and learn. David sorts out his knee by having Mark adjust his back, neck and jaw, demonstrating the wonders of kinesiology - where the pain is, it is not. I have a long chat with David about balancing the spiritual, emotional and rational and clearing the blockages formed by one's upbringing. It is a philosophical discussion on whether we live in a more tolerant society or not. Richard is dressed in pressed whites today, only needs a headscarf and could have been on the Haj. Mixed emotions, vacant mind, grounded. Isolated villages, interesting viaducts and buildings. The journey is a challenge, yet collaborative.

Day four

Road, wonderful church, triptych - time to think, muse, anger, the joy of the open empty mind - cars rushing by - churches built in a bygone age - monasteries, sacred relics - thousands of footsteps have gone before, following on sacred ground, guided by the spirit that carries us through life. It is a privilege to be on life's rich journey - a pilgrimage becomes very personally focused and yet one must make room for other people, their vagaries, views, frustrations and the petulance of others - we are who we are, striving to know our inner selves better and not to be distracted by the constant babble of Spanish televisions and people who hardly stop talking long enough to breathe - life's rich tapestry, kids run wild, communities, close knit existence... all is well.

Day five

David has fallen by the wayside and decides not to walk - a long day of 37km to Sahagun, so a taxi is taking the bags. An extended day - the joy of hardship which from time to time we need to embrace. I need to change the parameters next year - walk in clearer space. I am as a man with a mission, to be a pilgrim. So often in life I've taken the easy option, we must answer to ourselves. Sometimes there are no shortcuts, I've lied, I've been deceitful. I need to fully appreciate the power of honesty, but on some occasions we are led by white lies - our human fabric is paper thin, our integrity questionable. We need to strive, to seek forgiveness, to seek a purity of thought - minds are like washing machines, constantly churning, forever on high speed, multi spin. Get beneath the gigantic waves and seek the calmer water. Some people in small towns and villages along the Camino live in a sheltered world, seemingly cut off from mainstream life, with no multiple stores or 24-hour shopping, mass is still held each evening at church, people extend courtesies to one another. Life has a tempo, minds have seasons, there is still time to connect to nature. Small holdings may have given way to large ones, but many of the fields still reflect their medieval antecedents and are a laid out and cultivated as they have been since ancient times with sugar, crops, and few animals apart from the occasional flock of sheep and some goats. Emotions rise, feelings seem to be accentuated – words and phrases repeat themselves, anger rises within, patience is tested, words spoken are possibly wrongly interpreted, resentments linger for no apparent reason until cleared by mass. 'Peace be with you', a wonderfully healing sentiment, so profound. I fear, I doubt, I wonder.

David didn't join us for the 37km. I am annoyed with him - he could have walked it, through the discomfort zone. 'Montezuma's revenge' affects me on the way into town - no tissues, no room for me, blisters playing up - a day of pushing oneself to the limits.

Day six

From Sahagun, a short day's walk to El Burgo Ranero – young, planted, watered trees - sandy pebble path. A 17km, a morning's walk - ideas are working overtime - a Sunflower Trust triathlon for example? A pilgrimage is a personal walk, we learn not to be judgemental. David and Richard go like hares, attempting to catch up. Blisters playing up, anal dysfunction clearing, looking forward to clean underpants, excellent lunch followed by the joy of a well-deserved rest.

160

AND THEN ANOTHER YEAR …

Day one

A long first day on Camino VI, the spirit soars but the body finds it difficult to cope with the weight of a pack up hill and down dale. David expectorates with some success and I frequently marvel at the attitude and motivation of my 70-year-old walking partner. The perspiration drips, tiredness sets in - the *bocadillos* (long flat, bread rolls with dried meat) for lunch are incredibly salty and leave me dehydrated in the afternoon sun. *Peregrinos* ebb and flow, some friendly, others lost in profound thought. The *peregrinos* menu is sustained by red wine, beer and chips - three courses for 10 euros. It's the end of the season, very few people around - tomorrow it's uphill all the way - a tough one.

Day two

Next came a difficult day on the Camino. David gets a lift. Dinner with Aussies from Brisbane at O Cebreiro - so bloody cold, a mountain village. We walked 8km straight up a hill, surreal. Possibly the most difficult, with one very big man going in for knee operation. No buildings on the way, but we see two birds of prey today and find excellent church hostelries; my body is aching, a mess, and there could be two days of rain. Life is challenging - a Michelangelo day - full of agony and ecstasy. The heating doesn't come on, it gets very cold, there is no hot water. I put on tracksuit bottoms, socks and t-shirt, but the room is cold and I lie awake listening to David clearing his lungs in the room next door.

Day three

As I come downstairs in the morning, the front door is locked and guarded by a labrador/mountain dog cross so I beat a hasty retreat. Foul coffee and a taxi driver who tries to charge us four times the going rate to take our bags on to Triacastela. We leave as the day dawns, blue sky, no clouds and an autumnal breeze. What joy - the world lies before us on both sides and we are both well aware of God's magnificent creation, an amazing vista unequalled on our walk to date. It is like walking on the top of a mountain and looking down on all sides below, a glorious day. We arrive at Triacastela where we find Casa David, our bags waiting and delightful rooms with an outside table and writing area. The sun shines and slowly dips behind the mountain at 6pm.

O Cebreiro was marked by an indifferent service and a joylessness second to none, but here we are in a cold, magnificent spot. A smile costs nothings yet brings joy to so many. The walk has been varied, David preferring downhill or the flat, whereas I can change gear when the need arises to go uphill. It is a damn good workout and great cardiovascular exercise. A chance to think, be grounded and hold in awe the wonder of creation for which we give divine thanks. The joy of just being is something we lose sight of in our modern lives, though we are shaken out of our pleasures every time we stop at a Spanish café - the television is always on, usually at full blast with nobody watching it.

No day is ever the same. We communicate with a few monosyllabic words in Spanish and body language - we acknowledge fellow pilgrims but rarely get into any form of meaningful conversation, perhaps because it's an invasion of our space. Dinner and eucharist after that critical shower and a change into something half decent to give thanks for each day. The need to stop and be grateful I am sure is inherent in all of us, rather than being driven by 'what's in it for me'.

In Triacastela there were children playing, happy families, a lot of *peregrinos* - hot water, heating, idyllic pleasures. A great day's walk finished by a whiskey and great night's sleep.

The penultimate day is tomorrow, via Samos monastery to Sarria.

Day four

The clocks go forward in Spain, and everywhere there's confusion. No breakfast restaurant is open. The manager has got my passport, so we have to wait. Then a walk out of town, like no other, two hours of uphill with packs. We leave David in a café and walk on and decide that he's more than likely to take a taxi to Sarria, the next village. To my relief he's there. We walk on in high spirits in the fraternity of being.

An excellent omelette lunch is called for in Sarria, the end of our pilgrimage. Others are arriving to join us to begin their pilgrimage, like life's rich cycle: one ends, the other begins. The sheer joy of having reached a great milestone in my life as quite by chance we find that we are staying in the same hotel that we stayed in before we started the Camino, as with life, dust to dust, ashes to ashes, we are drawn back by life's umbilical pull and complete the circle. Another day, another chapter will unfold but the shared relationship and experience with David has been second to none. I'm a bolshie bastard but he's remained mellow and calm throughout.

SOME REFLECTIONS ON THE CAMINO

Having scaled the heights of Bhutan in order to raise money for a deaf/blind centre for children and realising that the altitude nearly finished me off, I found that at 50 and after the flatness of the Fens, the Himalayan trek was exceedingly challenging on an ageing body. So I decided that I needed to find an alternative pursuit to raise money for the various charities that I had become involved in. Richard Youdale, the former Head at King's Ely, lent me a book by Nicholas Luard, *The Field of the Star*. The author had walked the Camino one week each year as a cathartic means of getting over the death of his beloved daughter from HIV/Aids, caught from a tainted blood transfusion. It touched the litmus.

A number of chums said that they would come on the Camino, but backed out for a variety of reasons. I had visions of an eclectic group of people walking/talking and breaking bread together, similar to Chaucer's tale, the *Wife of Bath*. I mentioned it to David Smout, the Bursar at Ely Cathedral, and he said that he would be only too happy to join me on my walk from Sarria to Santiago de Compostela, a distance of 125km. We would thus qualify as *peregrinos*, get a Latin certificate from the cathedral in Santiago and I would raise funds for the Phayao Women's Development Foundation in Thailand, helping young girls get three years' high school education rather than going into prostitution. David was a wonderful 'old school' gent with a wide gait and military bearing. I realised that I would never keep up with him so we agreed to stop every two hours for a coffee or water, which worked well. He set off from Sarria in pinstripe trousers and shirt with an Aussie Outback hat, much to the delight of a passing Irish

164

cyclist who nearly fell of his bike. We carried our packs and attended the *peregrinos* mass each evening in the towns we passed through, apart from Mellide where the squid got the better of David. Having walked the last week, we enjoyed it so much that we decided that we would walk the whole Camino from St Jean Pied de Port, spending a week walking each year for five years. We were joined by Mark and Richard who completed the quest with us. Others who joined us for vignettes included Liz, Susan, Marianne, Geoff and Jill.

David was ordained and brought a travelling host and eucharist, which was helpful every evening at eight o'clock before a *peregrinos* supper.

We're on the road to somewhere

Michael McMahon recalls the pleasures and pains of a 600-kilometre pilgrimage

SITTING on the terrace outside El Peregrino hotel in La Portela, I was suddenly overcome by a wave of sadness. I had been walking the Camino de Santiago for nearly three weeks; I had travelled more than 600 kilometres. For up to 12 hours every day, I had put one booted foot in front of the other on a path that had taken me through fog and snow, rain and mud, dust and heat.

I had stayed in crowded pilgrim hostels where the bunks in the snore-rattled dormitories were so close together that there was no room to stand between them; one had to clamber in — and out — over the end. I had spent a night on a narrow mattress butted up against five others that together covered the entire floor of a small room; we six sleeping-bagged strangers might just as well have been sharing the same bed. I had blisters that felt like hot coals on the tips of my toes and the balls of my feet, and my boots had rubbed away a patch of skin on the back of each ankle. For much of each day, my back, shoulders and neck ached under the weight of my rucksack. And late in the afternoon on Sunday, May 30, my spirits took a deep, sudden dip, when I looked at my map and something unsettling dawned on me: my pilgrimage was coming to an end. Despite all that pain and incon...

Hey there, pilgrim: McMahon walked for up to twelve hours a day, through fog, snow, rain and mud

I raised money over my six years of walking El Camino for a variety of charities, from 80-year-old ladies feeding slum kids in Brazil to El Shaddai in India. Mark raised funds for the Sunflower

Trust and Marianne money to send the King's Barbers to sing for a charity in Thailand. Our ethos was 'every little helps'.

I have walked the last week on two further occasions with friends and family who needed some space in their lives or who had come to a crossroads. The two high spots for me were finding no accommodation in Rabanal, apart from the Parador, and discovering it was David's birthday. Large quantities of Marques de Riscal and Caceres were consumed with a local stew and this was followed by a memorable mass where one was aware of a wonderful presence.

Clive, an osteopath, can't carry his sack as he has a bad back and his conversations are obviously carried out for him through his wife; he seems to be lovingly dominated by her, she speaks for him, they're both almost 60 yet she mothers and dominates him, 'tis nothing stranger than life. Richard is slightly off his demeanour and obviously resents the fact that he missed the dinner because 'that' man was there (Father Andrew) - reconciliation must surely start somewhere. Susan is pleasantly quirky and out to have a decent walking holiday. I feel a bit like a tour operator as I'm asked, 'what do we do next? I try and get across the fact that everybody is on his or her own pilgrimage and there is total flexibility in the day, though we usually meet for evening mass at eight o'clock followed by a *peregrinos* dinner in a local hostelry.

We all have needs and carry our crosses. Carrying a day-bag each day I find is something of a 'cop out', yet if one can lighten the load, nobody has ever said that pilgrims must be heavily loaded. I'm sure that in olden times the gentry brought their servants. The aches, pains and challenges all reconcile quite quickly yet the sense of fraternity and oneness with nature will, I am sure, last forever.

Dear Lord,

Thank you for guiding us along the path of life and being with us in our hour of need, for the suffering that we experience may we be better people, and show compassion and tolerance to those around us at all times. Your path is our path and although we fall by the wayside from time to time we are eternally grateful that you pick us up and carry us for part of our journey. You teach us to appreciate the power and energy of nature and the strength of friendship. Our grateful thanks.
Amen.

FRIENDS TO REMEMBER

Aniello Salicone

We meet many people in life and a few remain with us throughout, 'tis like a braided river and some people criss-cross our paths more than others. I met Aniello in Monrovia, Liberia - he was dressed in a dish-dash (white Arab male dress). I thought that he was an Arab who didn't have enough change to get into the departure lounge so I gave him what loose change I had and thereafter we talked. Our flight from Monrovia to Dakar was delayed for four-and-a-half hours, which was not surprising as most flights either didn't leave or suffered interminable delays. It transpired that Aniello was an Italian Catholic priest who had been in charge of the seminary in Liberia for 17 years and was now being forced to flee. I next heard from him as he was living in the Xaverian missionary house in North London where he veered from the straight and narrow and was then sent to an isolated monastery in Switzerland to think about the path he wanted and needed to take. I found him there by chance on the anniversary of his acceptance in the priesthood. He was alone and I took him for a memorable lunch followed thereafter by bi-annual lunches or dinners either in North Italy or South of Naples where he stayed with his sister. He still sends me the service times for his church in Chicago where he is based with the Xavian missionary fathers and now carries out healing services guided by the spirit which moves in mysterious ways.

John Logue - An inspired teacher

John sent me a round robin mailing for a one-day introductory course in kinesiology. It sounded interesting and I enlisted. John was a truly inspirational teacher and I decided to take the certificate and diploma courses part-time. He was a man on a mission as he had been diagnosed with a terminal viral heart condition for which there was no cure and kinesiology had extended his life. He wished to spread the gospel of kinesiology and I suggested hiring the conference centre at Buckfast Abbey and for two very happy years we ran courses there which I co-ordinated and he taught.

He lived life to the full and the memory of *Bohemian Rhapsody* blasting out after a very traditional English country church funeral was very much in keeping with his spirit and sense of fun, let's live, have fun and party. The show goes on.

Jack Temple - 1st July 1917 - 13th February 2004

This was my eulogy:

'When May asked me to say a few words today I felt humbled and privileged, I thought about death and about growth and the changes in our lives that Jack brought about.

We are here today to celebrate the life and work of that extraordinary man. He was inspired, and possessed the talent for healing and touched many lives from all walks of life throughout his wonderful life.

As I sat outside the Blasius in Germany last weekend, a church built on a pre-Christian meeting place to celebrate the rites of spring, I realised that Jack's mission was timeless, stretching back before Atlantis, a seeker of eternal truth which has been suppressed by science, and to save the church. To many he was a star, small yet light years ahead of us and shines brightest on us in our darkest moments. Casting a shaft of light on darkness, stars are part of the panoply of the universe, even though the seasons change, the stars remain constant.

Jack was a magnet to the sick and the dying, those interested in dousing and the plainly curious and cynical. I was fortunate to know Jack for a number of years. I remember the first time I met him, he was totally engrossed in on-going research, he grunted, asked a few nominal questions doused with his crystal and told me what had been wrong with me for the previous fifty years. Strapped some homeopathy on my leg, told me to come back in six weeks and gave me a bill on a scrap of paper for £30.

I was fascinated by his approach, read his book and came for a series of treatments as I'm sure many of you did. We became friends talking of far flung parts, the Middle East, India and beyond - passing spirits with a shared zest for life and an interest in stone circles and Atlantis.

Jack was to some a quirky figure, an eccentric. He questioned the medical system and found it severely lacking.

169

He taught us all to be more curious and not to accept the status quo - to push out the boundaries. To eat and drink organically where possible and live with passion. Anybody who saw Jack teach all day, could not help but be touched by his tireless energy. Carpe diem, seize the day, always came to mind. There was always a twinkle in his eye and he had a common sense approach to life - never taking fools lightly and had little time for poorly trained kinesiologists, of which I happen to be one.

His approach to healing was a constantly developing continuum and it was very difficult at times to stay abreast of his intellectual acumen.

Jack was a gardener, a self-trained healer, a guide, a friend. It was a blessing that he touched my life and many of our lives with his boundless enthusiasm.

Just before he died I spoke to Jack in hospital as I still felt he had work to do here, he'd promised me another 40 years; I wanted him to try some organic wine from Thailand. His grip was still strong as was his spirit to the end. He took his time to cross to the other side. We are like masted sailing ships on the horizon - there she goes. Here she comes.

To me Jack, above all else, was a messenger with a message for us all that we are losing contact with the rhythm of the seasons and the universal energies of the mother earth, the stars and the planets. This garden is a fitting tribute from May and Nash. May acted as a rock and respite for Jack and for a number of years he was able to come here and recharge and share his vision of a better world. We are indebted to our maker, for having crossed Jack's path, to

170

have shared his life and been touched by it. I'm sure that by now he's checking auras on the other side.

May his spirit live on, his legacy will never be forgotten. Light has returned to light, we all give thanks'.

Father Andrew Richards.

I met Father Andrew when he was appointed Chaplain at King's Ely. He had moved there from Rossall School in Lancashire with his wife, Bev, and their children.

Andrew was an inspirational priest, truly blessed with the spirit when he donned his clerical garb, and he could communicate with one and all. He once took me to the Crism service at Walsingham where Anglo-Catholic priests re-affirm their vows during Holy Week. It was the most marvellous spectacle of smells and bells with all the priests wearing barettas... it was very 'high'. Afterwards, he told me that at his college in Oxford all the priests were known by their mother's maiden names so he thereafter became Mo/Maureen and I became Glad/Gladys. On his illustrious journey in life he once crossed the bridge to the English College in Rome and back again.

We made a memorable trip to Buckfast and one of his chums recognised him from the English College, assuming that he was still Catholic and so the monks asked him to con-celebrate which he duly did.

Andrew broke the bounds of a typical priest, as he could hold his own in any social setting. He moved onto Wellington College and the Duke of York's School before retiring early to France as his life had been dogged by chronic illness.

PHAYAO WOMEN'S DEVELOPMENT FOUNDATION

Some 25 years ago, John Kelly, a friend in Thailand, contacted me whilst we were living in New Zealand and asked if I would help find sponsors for young girls from the north of Thailand so that they could get three years' high school education. The cost was £50 per year. He was doing this because he was aware that prostitution was the only option for girls without a high school education. The response grew over the years, and up to 650 girls were given an education, thanks to the remarkable efforts of John and others.

In 2002 I was talking to Ian Bushell in Chiang Mai. He was an ex-Gurkha, educated at Wells Cathedral School and keen to take Christmas choral music to northern Thailand. I promised to ask Ely Cathedral as any funds raised would go to the Phayao Women's Development Foundation. By chance, on my return, I met Paul Trepte, the cathedral's director of music, and friends in the local pub. He was supportive but getting a decision from the Dean and Chapter would take time.

One of those friends, Marianne Felter, came up to me afterwards and said that she was interested in discussing the idea further and would I have a drink with her that Wednesday. When we met she suggested sending the King's Barbers (ex-choristers from the school) to Thailand and asked me how much I needed to raise? I did a quick calculation for 20 boys and five staff. Flight tickets would cost around £700 per person and I would arrange accommodation at Harrow School and Prem School in northern Thailand. The cost would be approximately £25,000 and with that she wrote me a cheque for that amount, requesting anonymity.

172

Ian had arranged concerts in the Intercontinental hotel in Bangkok, the British Embassy, Payap Baptist University, Seven Fountains Catholic Church as well as at Prem School. The high spot for me were the Christmas carols on the stairs at the Intercontinental and singing with the hill tribe school, though there were many others. The boys were excellent ambassadors and sang with great gusto, raising sufficient funds to sponsor a number of girls.

In 2007, the British Ambassador approached John Kelly to see if the choir would return to raise funds especially for the sea gipsy school on Koh Lanta which had been demolished in the tsunami. Marianne agreed to guarantee the trip and would walk part of the Camino to raise funds and the Barbers undertook various fundraising activities.

We managed to sponsor more than 100 girls and the Barbers, who were ably led by Peter North, put their hearts and souls into the venture. I will always remember two young men who insisted on a Thai massage in Chiang Mai and I had to sit outside the curtain to ensure the pleasures offered were not too diverse.

The following year Liz and I visited some of the girls in Pong with John Kelly who kindly arranged for me to meet some of the girls I'd sponsored. We went to one simple teak house where fish bones were drying on a metal sieve nailed to the gatepost. These bones would add a little extra nourishment to a bowl of rice. The family were poor but they gave us their all, it was incredibly touching. Visiting another family, we sat outside on raised corrugated tin and spotted a washing machine still in its plastic cover. The parents was incredibly proud because it had been won in the local lottery but they had no electricity supply. The daughter told me about her school and the joys of study. She was obviously very bright and the downside for her was that every day she had to walk

12km there and back as there was no transport available. She longed for a bicycle.

We left and bought her a $12 Chinese bike. When she saw it she was overcome with joy.

Sadly, at a time of change in the government in Thailand and the demise of Shinawatra, John decided to stand aside from Phayao and focus on other philanthropic interests.

'THE DUMPSTERS'

I remember being in Phnom Penh in 2007 and seeing a family living on the pavement, the children were semi-naked and drinking from the storm water in the drain while their forlorn parents sat on cardboard. I thought this can't be right. Everybody has a right to clean water and shelter. On my return to the UK, I saw that the Royal Bank of Scotland was discussing whether its next MD should be paid £12,000,000 a year and I thought, the world's gone crazy.

I decided to raise money to give the street kids a chance and thus walked part of the Camino to raise funds to open a school and many of my chums supported me. I returned to Cambodia the following February to look at the various options for an English language school and soon realised that the level of corruption was second to none and the bribes required would soon soak up my funds. I was quite despondent but by then I had been asked to inspect three private schools before I left the country. I said that I would charge nothing but the owners could take me for lunch to discuss my findings, which they did.

At lunch I met the academic director, Brian Gray, who asked me what I wanted to do and I told him and explained the difficulties that I'd faced. He was very supportive and asked if we would like to visit a school that he was involved with in his free time and at weekends. It was for the children on the rubbish dumps and he could take us there at seven o'clock the following morning, which we were happy to do as our flight didn't leave until later in the day.

He picked us up as agreed and we visited the school. A magical place. The children were in uniform, looked at you directly and smiled. The teaching was basic but good. Vegetables were being grown and animals being tended. There was Banksy-type art on the walls. The stories they had to tell about their lives were mind-numbing. I was so impressed that I passed over the funds that I had raised to date and promised we would return, which we have done regularly over the years. I felt that I wanted to leave the children with a legacy as the number of international benefactors increased and the children's lives were placed on a firmer footing. I decided that I would try to imbue them with a love of music as that would be something that nobody could ever take away from them.

The children of CCH rehearsing for their concert. WILL BAXTER

Former dump children sing for their futures

A fundraising event for the Centre for Children's Happiness NGO promises song, dance and 51 dazzling little smiles

I asked a number of close friends to help. One was Murray Laurence, who is a freelance travel writer for *The Australian* newspaper. He lives in Sydney and his wife Maureen was trained as a music teacher. Another friend, Donald Williams, was the key man. He has conducted a number of church choirs in middle England and was brought up in a Salvation Army family, working in his early days as a Butlins Red Coat. He's a great man with wonderful personal and musical talents. Liz, my partner, joined us and played an important pastoral role in the team.

We all spent three weeks in Phnom Penh and I arranged for La Gasolina, a French restaurant with an extensive garden, to stage an evening of Khmer song and dance and Donald and company coached the 'Dumpster Chorale' who sang a selection of songs in English. The 'great and the good', including the American Ambassador, joined the audience and gave generously as the event had been well supported by the local media. The only downside was that the video shot by a local Khmer to be placed on YouTube was flawed and it was only due to the technical prowess of my nephew Adam Stevens in New Zealand that anything was salvaged and we could use it to raise further funds.

All my chums left on the Sunday morning and I had promised Mech Sokha, the school's founder, that I would take those that had participated for an ice cream and soda later in the day. When I got to the gated courtyard all the children were waiting for me in their best bib and tucker. Mech said that I would be taking all the children. I asked, how many? It was 140 so not just the 43 who had performed and I had just $300 in my pocket.

We walked into a prosperous part of town - I felt like the pied piper - and found a deli run by a very acidic French expat. I left the youngsters outside and asked her if she could feed a number of young people with ice cream and soda. She was initially reticent but soon warmed up and got into the spirit of it. My $300 was exceedingly well spent just to see the look on the faces. Liz and I always remember to take balloons or colouring pens for all the children every time we visit.

The school is aptly named the Centre for Children's Happiness (CCH), and Mech Sokha is now building a new community centre on the edge of the rubbish dumps in the district of Chung EK where a further 30 children from impoverished families who live on, or near, the dumps will be taught. The picture on the next page shows how building work was nearing completion when I visited in June 2016.

Before this visit, I launched another appeal for the 'Dumpsters of Phnom Penh' and in only two months raised $2,750. This money was given to Mech while I was in Cambodia and it has touched many lives and given a number of less fortunate youngsters a stepping stone in life. The $2,750 will meet the cost of providing a teacher at the community centre for one year, until June 2017, covering Khmer, mathematics, English and computing. The children will also be able to join in arts and skills clubs. I also paid the community centre's water and electricity for one year and covered the cost of teaching materials.

There continue to be a number of new developments and a vocational training centre has been established in Sihanoukville so that a students can acquire further life skills after they leave CCH. It's a ray of light in a country with a dark past.

I am surrounded by happy 'dumpsters'.

AND FINALLY...

As I wrote earlier, it's always difficult to know where to start with a life story and my mind had been blocked for two weeks when I suddenly realised that I was trying to write from the head rather than the heart. Inspiration is like the rain, as the Arabian saying goes; it is the same for all human beings and yet it produces thorns in the marsh and flowers in the garden. I feel as though over the years I have built one brick wall after another around my heart and am growing aware that wisdom occurs when one drops the barriers that have been erected through one's concepts and conditioning.

Change occurs through awareness, like a sail boat with a full head of wind, moving effortlessly, just needing steering. Finally I have slowed down and can taste, smell and hear and allow my senses to become alive.

It is important to give up one's dependency and tear away the tentacles of society that have enveloped and suffocated one's being. Get back to nature, be grounded, enjoy the rhythm of the seasons. So many of us have empty, soulless lives because we crave popularity, appreciation and praise and have lost contact with sunsets, good books and good movies, enjoyable work and good company. People are influenced by the label, the power of the name, whether in shopping or in a position. We hate what we fear.
The day you cease to travel you will have arrived!

Here are some useful quotes I have collected from various sources:

Spring has past, summer has gone and autumn is here and the song that I meant to sing remains unsung. Most people do die with the great song of their lives remaining unsung.

There is a wick within you that is waiting to become the light of your soul. When the inner flame burns brightly you will feel a magnificent awakening in your life.

We spend our lives chasing the elusive pot of gold, only to discover that our best treasures were the ones that we always had but never knew.

Life is too short to be too little.

Live in the curiosity, live in the awe, live in the wonder.

Shift from condemnation to compassion and from complicity to simplicity.

Keep the gold and keep the silver, but give us wisdom.

Death is not the greatest loss in life, the greatest loss is what dies inside us whilst we live.

The most pathetic person in the world is someone who has sight but no vision.

Leave a legacy, the deepest longing for the human heart is the need to live for a cause greater than himself.

The meaning of life is to serve the force that sent you into the world, then life becomes a joy.

Made in the USA
Charleston, SC
24 September 2016